Frederick O Layman

Maximilian I. A conflict between the Old World and the New.

Tragedy in four acts

Frederick O Layman

Maximilian I. A conflict between the Old World and the New. Tragedy in four acts

ISBN/EAN: 9783743328419

Manufactured in Europe, USA, Canada, Australia, Japa

Cover: Foto ©ninafisch / pixelio.de

Manufactured and distributed by brebook publishing software
(www.brebook.com)

Frederick O Layman

Maximilian I. A conflict between the Old World and the New.

Tragedy in four acts

DRAMATIS PERSONÆ.

MAXIMILIAN, *Archduke of Austria; later Emperor of Mexico.*
DOCTOR BASCH.
FATHER VISCHER.
AGUIRRE, }
CAMPOS, } *Maximilian's Ministers.*
LARES, }
MEJIA, (Pronounce, Me-heé-a). }
MIRAMON, } *Maximilian's Generals.*
MARQUEZ, (Pronounce, Már-kes). }
LA BASTIDA, *Archbishop of Mexico.*
ALMONTE.
NAPOLEON III., *Emperor of France.*
DRUYN DE LHUYS, *Minister.*
LULU, *Prince Imperial of France.*
BAZAINE, *French Generalissimo.*
AGUILAR.
JUAREZ, *President of the Republic of Mexico.* (Pronounce, Huár-ez).
PORFIRIO DIAZ, }
ARTEAGA, (Pronounce, Ar-te-á-ga) } *Juarez's Generals.*
SALAZAR, }
PRINCE ITURBIDE.
A SCHOOLMASTER.
EUGENIE, *Empress of France.*
CARLOTTA, *wife of Maximilian.*
DONNA ARTEAGA, *the General's wife.*
DONNA INEZ, *her daughter, betrothed to Salazar.*
PRINCESS ITURBIDE.
DONNA MEJIA.

Courtiers, Peasants, Soldiers, Servants, Workmen, Etc.

ACT I.

Scene I. *Library in the Tuileries.*

Napoleon III. *Later his* Body Servant.

Napoleon [seated at his work table].
That is the plan, arisen from the haze
Of doubt and hesitation; that will do.
For every case that I can think of now
I plainly see my way; see how it winds
Through difficulties, failures and delays
Until it leads me to the glorious goal,
And for the unexpected turns of fate
I see a by-way for a safe escape.

Jean. The night has passed, the sun is rising bright,
And yet your Majesty has had no rest.
Indeed, I fear the public welfare is
Too dearly bought with your imperial health.

Napoleon. Thanks, good old Jean, for all your honest care;
But work that ripens and promotes our plans
Refreshes more than dead and heavy sleep;
And moderation, both in sleep and meals,
Gives us a mental strength that well befits
A monarch watching over Europe's peace.
I feel so strong to-day that with this hand
I could destroy and crush a mighty realm
To reconstruct it on a better plan.

Jean [*he extinguishes the light and opens the curtains*] *aside.*
For heaven's sake! this waking over night
Is just what causes all these frightful plans.
Is France this realm, this smoking powder keg,
That must be crushed to atoms from above,
Before they blow it skyward from below;
Or is it but poor, suffering Mexico
That now for months has cost us men and means,
To teach the savage Indians how to spell?
What do I care! I dance with all the rest
In this wild chaos, the imperial court,
And, taking all in all, I can't complain. [*Exit.*

Napoleon. What labyrinth! How wonderful the threads
Of past events are woven into one
Mysterious cloth called History; that wraps
In deep oblivion our origin.
The poet's bold imagination can
Create no picture half so strange and weird
As painted by the hand of History.
The humble lawyer's son an emperor,
Who weds a princess; conquers mighty realms
And lavishly bestows them on his friends,
While he rules wisely on the throne of France;
Then, suddenly, his lucky star goes down;
Reverses follow him at every step
Until a prisoner of war he dies,
Forgotten and alone on desert isle.
The Moscow cinders barely cease to glow—
That greatest death-torch of the greatest man—
When wife and child lie mouldering in their graves;

And gone is all the power of his kin;—
Until in me the dynasty revives, —
A wonderful relation! And the end—
Ah! how I wish that I might live to see.   [*Sunshine*.
But no! Away with all these gloomy thoughts,
Wild echoes of the phantoms of the night.
Here! Jean, a glass of wine, my very best!
And then to work such as the day may bring.
    [*He drinks the wine. Newspapers, etc., are brought in.*
                  Looking into the latter].

Still criticising, grumbling, crying out,
Still rattling at the gates of government,
And where, with fear, I give one privilege,
The unrelenting mob demands ten more.
No; fullest freedom should be mine alone,
For, like the wine which fortifies the wise
And strengthens them to noble words and deeds,
But drives the crowd to misery and crime;
So, likewise, does unguarded liberty.
Such wine of freedom multitudes can bear
But in a very moderate degree.
What were those bloody revolutions but
Intoxication caused by freedom's wine?
Then the Republic, sober, weak and dull,
The seedy morning of that freedom's brawl—
I know the vaults, built in the far off west,
Where they ferment that thrice accursed wine.
Shopkeepers are they all, and their conceit—
A mercenary people's sovereignty—
Is punished justly by fraternal war.

What if the lucky moment had arrived
When I could draw advantage from their plight,
Forever check that proud republic's strength,
And build anew a throne to monarchy.
Yes, that would stop the ever greedy mouths,
Of editors—instead of freedom's wine ——

SCENE II.

EUGENIE. NAPOLEON.

Eugenie [*who has heard the last words*].
Give them an opiate draft of France's *gloire;*
The slumbering man is managed easily,
While the intoxicated will revolt;
The pupil bows before the master mind.

Napoleon. Ah, excellent, my well instructed queen
And very worthy partner of my throne!
How did you rest; and how is our good prince?

Eugenie. The prince is well and he will soon be here.
What is the news? [*She points to a map of Mexico which lies on his desk at the left, seating herself to the right.*]

Napoleon [*going to and fro*]. The very best, madame.
In Mexico the troops have great success;
And Juarez yields, the wily fox gives in.
I wish we did as well in Austria!
There is no better head for that new state,
Than Archduke Maximilian would make.
I do not see why he should hesitate.
[*Ironically.*] He was the choice of Mexico's free men.

They offer an imperial crown. And he,
Instead of seizing it with outstretched hands,
Demands to hear once more the people's voice!
For what again this idle puppet play—
At least—I mean—the play with votes of men
Who cannot always be relied upon.

Scene III.

The same. Lulu.

Lulu. Papa, Papa! can I go riding now?

Napoleon. My darling child! No. When your work is done.

Eugenie. I think 'tis calculation in the Prince,
He wants to free himself from all reproach
And bind your troops more firmly to his throne.

Lulu. Can I go now!

Napoleon. No, no, my dearest boy.
When you have learned your lesson; not before.
[*To her.*] No. I believe he has a noble heart;
He is not shrewd, but has good common sense;
He knows the world, yet is a dreamer, too.
All that just makes him serve my purpose well.
[*To the child.*] Don't touch the things upon the table, son.
[*To her.*] The second delegation, just arrived
From Mexico, will be received to-day,
And sent to Miramare with my pledge.

Eugenie. May I be present?

Napoleon. Certainly, madame.

You know how much I value your advice,
And doubly where the clergy is concerned.
'Tis queer that priests and women should agree;
For pretty women shun all serious work,
And priests should hate whatever smacks of love.

Eugenie. O, Sire, it ill becomes a noble prince,
To joke and laugh at our most sacred faith.

Napoleon. I do not laugh, but wonder why it is.
Well, well; the striving pupil may, in time,
Rule wiser than the master does to-day.
Now go; perfect your toilet, and be sure,
You choose a dress to please the bishop's taste.

[*Exit Eugenie.*

Scene IV.

Lulu. Napoleon.

Lulu. Papa, what is that here? [*He climbs on a chair and looks at the map.*]

Napoleon. That city there?
Why you should tell your father what it is,
If you had studied your geography.

Lulu. O, there! it says, I think, Me-x-i-co.

Napoleon. Well, now you see ——

Lulu. Is that the town
That they will call "New Moscow" after this?

Napoleon [*angrily*].
What do you mean! Where do you hear such talk?

Lulu [*frightened*].
The Marshal's son, with whom I played last night;
He saw it in a journal, so he said.

Napoleon.   Such papers are not made for boys like you;
Devote yourselves to good instructive books.
Go, go my son, and let those things alone.

Lulu.   O, Papa, do not scold.   [*Exit.*

Napoleon.   New Moscow?   Hm!

Scene V.

The Tuileries.   Throne Room.

Servants and Workmen.

1st Servant.   Well, are you ready, for your time is up?

Carpenter [*at work on the throne*].
Yes, yes.   I'll draw the velvet over here
And nothing will be seen of hole or spot,
There—I have done.

2d Servant.   You call that honest work,
To cover up what ought to be repaired?

Carpenter.   From olden times, the purple covered up,
So many little rotten spots and things——

1st Servant.   Man, are you mad to talk like that at court!
And is it proper for a journeyman,
Who made a pretty penny near the throne?

Carpenter.   O, that is quite original.   You see
I am a Frenchman of the rough, old school
And do not creep, where I must make my gain.

1st Servant. A wicked mouth. He'll talk himself some day
Right into prison.

2d Servant. But it's fun to hear.

Carpenter. Well, brothers, be that as it may
I know much more than I can say.
I'm court repairer, and I mend
The little cracks that time will rend.
I know the benches and the banks;
Know when they'll break from pranks of cranks.
I know how hard an emperor's bed;
I know how thin the cord or thread
That binds the subject's faith. I've pried
Below the covers where they hide;
I sewed the curtains, gold and red,
In which the curtain lecture's read.
I get supports and find new roles,
When throne or pulpit's full of holes.
I know the role and fate of Lulu's reign—
And I prefer two bottles of champagne. [*Enter Jean.*

Jean. Come, hurry up. The court will soon arrive.

SCENE VI.

DRUYN DE LHUYS [*from the left.*

Druyn. "To hope the best and to expect the worst,
Renews the courage and prevents conceit;"
So says his Majesty—quite vague and curt.
"Good luck, in foolish hands, may do much harm;
Bad luck, in wise men's hands may turn to good."

Such proverbs are for children!—that, to me.
Here are the Mexican ambassadors
And no one saw them but the Emperor.
What do they bring? Good luck, or is it bad?
Is it the best "that we should always hope?"
Is it the worst "that we should now expect?"—
And yet, alas, I must receive the court,
Must smile or frown; must show a policy.
If I could see the Archbishop in time!
A letter came for him from Mexico. [*He goes to window.*

Scene VII.

Druyn, La Bastida, Almonte, and attendants.

Almonte. The letter which you got through Aguilar ——

La Bastida. Contains but empty words and nothing more.
I know no more than any man in France—
I am ashamed to come to court like that;
How will it look if we are not *au fait?*

Almonte. If we could see the Minister of State
He might give information.

La Bastida. Yes— but still —
We must proceed with caution. Otherwise,
He might find out how little ——

Almonte. Why, of course.

Druyn. It is enough to make a fellow mad. [*Stamps.*

Almonte. Who's talking? Ah, a very happy chance.

Druyn. Be welcome, gentlemen.

La Bastida. My friend, be blessed.

Almonte. You issued from the Emperor's boudoir?

Druyn. Well,— yes,— some time ago. A lovely day!

La Bastida. The fairest wind for our high embassy.

Druyn. Yes. They arrived. I think they had for you
A letter, which I hope you have received?

Almonte. His worship did receive a letter; yes.

La Bastida. { What is the news?
Druyn. { Well, how do matters stand?

La Bastida. I beg your pardon.

Druyn. Honored Father, speak.

La Bastida.
You are the Emperor's mouth, speak you the first.

Druyn. You are the guests, and I defer to you.
What are the chances in the far-off west?

La Bastida. They write — but — I will not anticipate.
You were about to say —

Druyn. Why stand on form.
I pray, quite *sans façons.*

La Bastida. I am all ear.

Druyn. No, no; I mean the letter, you received.

La Bastida. A modest reticence becomes a priest.
Proceed.

Druyn [aside]. No use. [*Aloud*]. Well, gentlemen, you see,
Affairs have got into a novel state ——

Almonte. Of course, a state ——

La Bastida.   A new one I admit.
Druyn [*perspiring*].   A state that is ——
Herald.   The Emperor!
Druyn.   Thank God.

SCENE VIII.

The same. NAPOLEON. EUGENIE. Court. AGUILAR.
And Deputation from Mexico.

Napoleon. It is again my privilege to speak
To you, my friends and Councilors of State,
To give the reasons for imperial acts
As far as foreign politics permit,
And to receive from you that sound advice
That ever leads me for the people's best.
The throne of France rules not alone at home.
No. It protects the Frenchman everywhere.
Injustice that was dealt in Mexico
To strangers; and among them Frenchmen, too,
Called forth the noble fleet that bore the crews
Of France, of England and of Spain. But lo!
No sooner had an insufficient pledge,
And meager ransom-money been obtained,
Than England's men-of-war and Spain's, withdrew.
The government that rules the British Isles
Is not inspired by military fame,
As that of France. She sees her glory through
The unclean spectacles of trade and gain,
Just as she sees her sun through dismal fog;

And Spain called back her troops because at home
They lack the great security and wealth
That we enjoy in this our blessed realm.
And so we stood alone in foreign lands,
Outnumbered largely by rebellious hordes,
And, as on Solferino's battle-field,
The eyes of all the world were fixed upon
The troops of France, all eager for the fray.
Was I to do as my allies had done,
And trust that Indian chief's contemptuous word;
"He would accord the French as many rights,
As much protection as all foreigners?"
Was I to break my bravest Marshal's staff
And damp the courage of my officers,
Teach the recruits a cowardly retreat,
Before they ever saw a victory?
Was I to call the navy home in fear;
The laughing stock of both the hemispheres?

    [*Murmurs beginning during the last sentences and growing, bursts forth.*

    Court. No. Forward! Forward! At the Enemy!

    Napoleon. "Aye, Forward!" so said I, and forward went
The brave, victorious troops from place to place,
Till from the capitol and every spire,
The *tricolor* of France in triumph waved.
And, free from all the pressure of revolt
The people's sound convictions showed themselves
With dignified, unanimous consent;
They voted for imperial government,
And as the first to wear the crown, they chose
My friend, the Archduke Maximilian.

Scene IX.

The same. Later, the Minister.

Servant. The Minister from the United States
Of North America is waiting, Sire,
And urgently requests that he be heard.

Napoleon. How! Can the lion roar that bleeds to death
From self-inflicted wounds. Yes. Call him in.
Their stubborn pride of weakness I would see.

Embassador. The government of the United States
Sends cordial greeting to your Majesty.

Napoleon. The same to all your States. Well, honored Sir,
What is your message? Is it war or peace?

Embassador. Is that indifferent to your majesty?

Napoleon. I wish for peace but never fear a war.

Embassador. Sire, if you truly wish for peace, you will
Respect the nation's rights and cease to crush
With cannon and with sword, the liberties
Of that poor, suffering race of Mexico,
That now is writhing in enslaving chains.

Napoleon. Because I always honor people's rights
I ask that mine should be respected too;
And I revenge on those rebellious hordes
The wrong they did to those whom I protect.

Embassador. The injury—if such was done to France—
Has fully been repaired. And Juarez, Sire,
Whom here you class with rebels, he is called

In Washington, the rightful president.
The States will never recognize a throne
Supported but by foreign bayonets.

Napoleon. And those called rebels, now at Washington,
We call defenders of their liberty.
To preach the right of nations, ill becomes
Those who, in bloody fratricidal war,
Are throttling freedom in their brother States,
Because from loathsome Union they would part.

Embassador. Yes, from a Union that they vowed to keep.
And for what reason did they draw the sword?
That they, in disregard of human rights,
Might fatten on the curse of slavery.

Napoleon. What laws and customs justified till now
Is called at present vile, inhuman crime.
It suits your tyranny in freedom's mask!

Embassador. May both our acts be judged by history.
What message shall I send to Washington?

Napoleon [*with deliberation*].
You may report I value their advice,
But their example would impress me more.
If they will recognize the Southern States,
And thereby show that in the western world
The people's rights are fairly recognized,
I will, with pleasure, follow in their lead,
And will withdraw my troops from Mexico.
If not, I shall construe a nation's right
Exactly as they do themselves, and fight.

Embassador. So I will state. [*Exit.*

Napoleon.   What says my council now?
And what say you? [*to Druyn.*]

   Druyn.   May I still hesitate?
Proud was the word and worthy of a prince
But was it not too hard?   Consider it,
If now, perchance, the States conclude a peace,
And with united armies should enforce
The haughty words of their Embassador?
No doubt our troops would easily repulse
Such mobs as fight in North America;
But yet the country that needs speedy rest,
Would see for many years more blood and steel.
It seems to me, perhaps, the wisest move
To leave this far-off Mexico in peace;
So that the government, now well installed,
May gain in time the people's confidence.

   Napoleon [*aside*].   "New Moscow" rings forever in my ear!

   Almonte.   No, do not listen to your Minister,
Who rates the honor of great France so low,
That he would let those untamed rebels crush
Again, the glorious, but half-finished work.

   La Bastida.   O say a word, beloved Empress, speak
In favor of the Holy Father's cause.

   Eugenie.   I, too, beseech you, my imperial spouse,
To follow the dictations of your soul.
Though wisely our good minister may warn,
To well consider and to move with care,
An Emperor should act with firm resolve
Where he, in duty bound, must keep his word.

Remember that this war serves not alone
To benefit the men of Mexico.
No, for the power of the Latin race,
For our belief and for the Holy See,
The troops are fighting for the Roman Church.

  La Bastida. Ha! what a wife! an angel sent from heaven!
The holy Father blesses you through me.

  Napoleon. Be not alarmed, no threatening frightens me.
The eagle's cry sounds like the raven's caw
When lame his wings, and when his vicious claws
Are buried in his body's flesh and blood,
And nothing but the beak seems undestroyed.
Go, La Bastida and Almonte, both,
To Mexico, as soon as you can leave.
There seize at once the reins of government
And hold them firmly, till they pass from you
Into my noble friend, the Emp'ror's hand.
You start for Miramare, Aguilar;
The Archduke will—he must—accept the crown
That rightly has belonged to him for months.
  [*Stepping between La Bastida and Almonte.*]
The man whose arm is braced by right and might
And heaven's help, is sure to win the fight.

Scene X.

Miramare.   Castle Gardens.

MAXIMILIAN and CARLOTTA.

  Carlotta. Come, Max, and leave those dreary volumes. See!
How lovely our dear Miramare is,

When from the buds and from the joyful birds
The scents and sounds of spring are breaking forth.
You used to praise the glorious fields and woods;
You said, upon the mountain, men could learn
Far more than from thick books in dusky rooms;
And now you sit at home; you read and write,
And hardly see your garden or your wife.

   Max. Yes, yes. You are quite right. How times have changed.

   Carlotta. Are you not happy, Max, as formerly?

   Max. Yes, happy any man with such a wife,
Though he might live in icy North-pole's night.

   Carlotta. O, go along! We're no more bride and groom!

   Max. And should I love you less on that account?

   Carlotta. No, no! but spare the compliments. Now come.

   Max. Well, I am ready; where are we to go?

   Carlotta. Up to the little forest. To the spot
Where I would like to build a summer-house.
I first saw Miramare from that point
In all its glory, and so there it is
I want to go next summer, sit and dream.

   Max. Next summer, child, we may be far from here.

   Carlotta. You talk in riddles, Max; I often fear
That cares are on your mind. Confess to me,
That I may share in all your troubles, dear.

   Max. Beloved wife! Yes, you should know it now.
Come in this arbor; I will tell you all,
And why I kept it secret all along.
You see, I feared it might disturb your peace.

The doctor told me that your little heart
Was made for love and joy, but not for care;
Expecting, anxious hoping, and perhaps
Resigning, would be poison for your nerves.

 Carlotta. The naughty doctor; I will scold him well.

 Max. You know, that when a youth, I was in Spain.

 Carlotta. So you have told me many times before.

 Max. I did not tell, however, what occurred
So ominously at Granada once.
The day had been quite sultry, and the night
Sank dark and chilly on the sleeping town.
Stretched on my bed I lay, but could not sleep;
I thought of all that I had seen and done.
The old cathedral, I so much admired
The day before, arose before my eyes,
In all its grand and mystic pomp arrayed;
And near the chapel, where the swords and crowns
Of Emp'ror Francis lie in safe confine,
The image of the Virgin Mary stands,
Bedecked with jewelry and precious stones.
In vain I tried to tear my mental eye
Away from this one portion of the church;
I stared until my tired eyelids burned.
It seemed as if the Holy Virgin called,
And gently bent her lovely head to me.

 Carlotta. While dreaming or awake?

 Max.   I do not know—
The wishes of the heart the eye will paint
On night's dark background, then absorb again

The self-drawn picture, and impose it as
Reality upon the dazzled mind.
And stronger grew my wish; I felt impelled
So urgently that I could not resist.
I threw my heavy cloak around my neck,
And walked, until upon the moonlight square
I stood before the grand and sombre dome.
The night air had refreshed my throbbing brain,
And so I entered, serious but composed;
The Holy Virgin stood immovable,
Enlivened only by a flickering lamp.

    Carlotta. How wonderful! I'm all excitement, Max.

    Max. How long I stood before the iron bars,
That serve to guard the Spanish Hapsburg's crown,
I could not say. But in my heart I felt
The burning wish to conquer with my sword,
Some future day, a glorious crown like his.
I pressed my feverish head against the bars——

    Carlotta. What happened then? I feel all hot and cold!

    Max. And presently I heard a mighty roar
That softened to mysterious murmurings.
I saw the Virgin's lips—they seemed to move—
And heard, enchanted, these prophetic words
That I shall nevermore forget.

    Carlotta.   You heard——

    Max. She said to me—"A Monarch thou shalt be;
A mighty kingdom is awaiting thee!"
I fainted on the marble—and to-day——

Carlotta. Well, what to-day? I dressed myself so gay
Because you wished it; but I knew not why.

Max. To-day I am to have that crown at last;
The State of Mexico has chosen me.

Carlotta. Is this reality, or still a dream?

Max. They offered me the crown some time ago,
But I mistrusted their proceedings then.
I wished once more to test their honest vote,
While I might pray for guidance from above;
And, therefore, I concealed it all from you.
But Aguilar is soon expected here
To tender me the crown a second time.
I will not hesitate, but seize the prize,
And the Madonna's words will be fulfilled.

Carlotta. Then you, my Max, will be an Emperor;
And I, a child, will be an Empress then.
O think of all the good that we can do!

Max. I know you can and will do good, my love.

Carlotta. But Mexico! How far, how far away!
And separated by so vast a sea,
From home; and Belgium, too!

Max. O do not cry,
My dearest wife; for at my side you will
Soon find abroad a new and happy home,
And spreading joy, you will yourself rejoice.

Carlotta. O leave me to collect my wandering thoughts;
I am confused, it came so suddenly.

Max. Behold our friends. Go with the Countess Thun;
Walk up and down and cool your heated brow.

Scene XI.

[*In the meantime servants have lighted the garden.*]

The same. Count and Countess Thun. Later Dr. Basch.

Max. God bless you, Count. What do you bring from France?

Count Thun. The Emp'ror's greetings and his guaranties.

Max. Be doubly welcome with such happy news!
O what a man this Emperor; as keen
In his ideas as mighty in his deeds;
Unselfish in his friendship, staunch and true.
How I do wish that I could press his hand
Before I start to cross the ocean's depth.   [*Enter Basch.*
Here, Doctor! Do you look for me?

Basch [*giving him a letter*].   Why yes;
This letter from his Majesty, just came.
[*To Thun*].   Well, Count; when will the delegates be here?
          [*They talk while Max. reads the letter.*]

Thun. I am expecting them at any time.
And do you go with us to Mexico?

Basch. My proper place is by my Emp'ror's side,
As true and firm as by the Archduke's now.

Max. My worthy Doctor, spoken like a man.
My brother warns. He fears the French may fail;
Advises me to stay; he does not know
What is the friendship of a Bonaparte.

No; I have faith like you, Count Thun; and you.
Now, tell me frankly, Doctor; do you hold
My brother's views, or do you share my own?

Basch. The views of both, my prince. No doubt it is
A dang'rous undertaking. But for that
A Hapsburg does not hesitate to act.
A doctor does not ask about the risks
That his profession forces him to run;
He goes to help and trusts in Providence.

Max [*smiling*]. How good; how wise—and diplomatic too;
 [*In the meantime more guests of the Queen enter.*]
Be welcome, you, and you; and you, dear friends;
The last time here on Miramare's shores. [*Enter Servant.*

Servant. The delegates from Mexico.

Carlotta [*hurrying to him*]. O Max!
The time has come.

Max. Are you prepared?

Carlotta. I am!

Scene XII.

The same. AGUILAR and others of the Embassy.

Aguilar. Again we dare approach your majesty
And place the hope and welfare of a race
With humble prayer in your princely hands;
For you alone can save our ruined land.
The members that in wild and headless war

Inflicted on each other bloody wounds,
Rest now exhausted, but unreconciled.
In you we found the head that can control
The warring factions and secure us peace.
So that the bleeding body, our poor land,
May, step by step, recover; and at last,
Through education and by steady work,
Will grow to be a mighty kingdom soon.

Max. [*aside*].
"A mighty kingdom;" yes, those were the words!

Aguilar. O, do not turn us back in hopeless grief;
Do not reject the better class of men
For what a band of reckless rebels did.
Take here this parchment with the nation's vote,
That shows the honest wish of Mexico;
And in that people's name we offer you,
Prince Maximilian, Duke of Austria,
The sceptre and the crown of Mexico.   [*Gives him the roll.*

Max. And I, by this, accept the glorious crown,
For now I understand the voice of Fate.
The crown shall be a helmet on my head,
A sword of judgment shall my sceptre be,
Until the rebel hordes are all subdued.

Carlotta. But then your crown shall turn into a wreath,
The sceptre turn into a shepherd's staff,
And pardon take the place of iron law.
Hearts swayed by fear alone are filled with hate;
What sword and shackles never will attain,
The people's love, with mercy we will gain.

Max. So shall it be! And now my honored guests
Come to the palace, where a gay repast
Will help us to forget the parting hour;
And you, my friends, who go with us abroad,
Bid now good-by to friends and house and home,
For soon the word is: "Ho! for Mexico!"

END OF FIRST ACT.

ACT II.

Scene I.

Mejia's valley in Mexico. To the right, Arteaga's cottage; to the left, Mejia's house; in the center, a wedding feast. ARTEAGA *and* WIFE, SALAZAR *and* WIFE, DONNA MEJIA, SCHOOLMASTER, Guests, *etc., etc.*

Donna Arteaga. And so you saw the Emperor yourself?

Donna Mejia. But for a moment, as they swiftly passed,
He and the Empress in an open coach;
And from the eyes of both beamed love and joy.
And right behind their carriage, in great pomp,
Sat on a prancing horse—who do you think?—
Mejia!

Donna Arteaga. Can it be!

Donna Mejia. As General!

Schoolmaster. Congratulations for the bride's mamma,
And for the new-made Mrs. Gen'ral, too.

Donna Arteaga. Behold! here is the master of the school;
How glad I am that you have found your way,
Through all the warlike dangers everywhere,
To celebrate with us this festal day.

Schoolmaster. Great science stands above the partisans;
Her followers go free through martial crowds,

Because, you see, the principle is this:
On men like me, who are in knowledge rich,
No further worldly wealth is ever sought;
So that, with, through and by, this want of coin,
The great advantage is upon our side;
And that, indeed, perhaps, in consequence——

Donna Arteaga.
There; save up something for the wedding speech.

Inez [*hidden from the others by bushes*].
My Salazar! at last you are my own!
O how I wish that we were all alone,
And all festivities were past and o'er.
How hard they make the road to happiness,
With eating, dancing, talking and what not.
Here I must laugh; there I must hug and kiss,
From sheer enjoyment one cannot enjoy.

Salazar. Have but a little patience, dearest wife,
And we will change the gay and noisy scene
For happy, quiet, dreamy solitude.

Arteaga. Where is that couple?—always hid away!

Salazar. I knew it. Here we are!

Arteaga. Come to the feast.
[*They seat themselves.*] Your glasses fill, and for a little while
Lend to my simple words a friendly ear.
A vet'ran soldier, and a farmer now,
I work much better with my arms and hands
Than with my mouth. But on this gala day,
As father of this happy, little bride,
I will attempt to find words to express

The wishes and intentions, that for both,
Since many months lay hidden in my heart.
The man who weds my Inez on this day
Has fought in many battles by my side;
And more than once I owe my life to him.
Then, when I got this land, a cloister farm,
Deserted by the monks, he helped to turn
The dismal desert into what you see,
With all the troubles in a time of war.
And now that we expect a speedy peace,
Assured by strong imperial government,
I give this man my blessing, with my child,
And all the farming land.

    Salazar.   Not all your farm!

    Arteaga.   Yes, all is yours; for my declining strength
The garden and the fruit is quite enough.

    Inez.   Oh, father, mother, that is far too much!

    Donna Arteaga.   Live long and well, and happy on the farm.

    Guests.   Long may they live!

    Schoolmaster.   Allow a friend to speak.

    Guests.   Aha! Now listen; so you don't get lost.

    Schoolmaster.   If I particularly think of him,
Who, indirectly, by his glorious deeds,
Has helped to bring about this wedding feast;
It is because I stood so near to him—
I speak here of the Emperor—for I—
Commanded the reception to assist—
Advanced with hundred children to the shore,
To strew the path with flowers and hurrahs!——

Salazar.   Indeed, we owe the Emperor great thanks.

Schoolmaster.   And afterwards—I do not say, because—
But still, perhaps, in some connection, I
Discovered hundred dollars in my pouch.

Arteaga.   That was not much for such exciting work.

Schoolmaster.   Now, don't you see, where such enormous sums
Are sacrificed to scientific art;
That is a sign, that peace is near at hand.
So that, at once, in jubilirious joy,
We plunge into the waves of sentiment,
And drink long life to "Emperor and Peace!"

All.   Hurrah for Emp'ror Max!

Scene II.

The same.   JUAREZ and PORFIRIO.

Juarez.   Who are these folks?

Porfirio.   The friends of Arteaga; he whose child
Has married Salazar this very day.
Both men have served with Santa Anna's force;
And, as I hear, with courage and much skill,
So that they soon advanced to higher ranks.

Juarez.   We need good leaders and the French are near.
Is it not possible to win those men?

Porfirio.   You never will.   Those people want repose;
And whether right or wrong rules in the land
They do not care; in fact they do not know.
The one is old, the other dead in love;

That makes them tame. Besides, Mejia is
Their friend; and he was honored with high trust.
You heard them shouting as we came along.
They are imperial men from top to toe.

Juarez. Mejia, traitor, you shall pay for this!
As to those men, I think you judge them wrong;
In every breast there is a spark of right,
And more so in a vet'ran soldier's heart;
Perhaps, with glowing words, I may succeed
In fanning that faint spark into a blaze.
Go you, Porfirio, watch the enemy—
It is so easy to surprise us here.   [*Exit Porfirio.*

Scene III.

The same, except Porfirio.

Juarez. Most worthy gentlemen and ladies fair,
Permit a poor and tired wanderer
A modest share in all this happiness.
A drink, a bite, a smile or friendly word,
And thankful I will go my lonely way.

Guest. A high-bred beggar man—what modest pride!

Arteaga. No sufferer goes empty from my door;
And if a friend of peace and Emp'ror Max,
You shall be welcome to my humble home.

Juarez. I am for peace and him who brings that peace,
Whoever he may be.

Arteaga.   Your soldier's dress,
Though, seems to contradict your peaceful words.

Juarez. And why? Not every man who favors peace
Can always live in peace. For every man
Must be defender of his property;
Must guard his house and home from vile attacks;
From being broken into over night.
A villain, who has driven me from home,
Who robbed and slew my children, is the man
I am in search of—wandering far and wide.
At times I go ahead with hope and cheer,
And then again retract the useless steps.
I will not rest until my arm has slain,
My foot has trodden him into the dust.

Donna Arteaga. What awful fate!

Inez. How sad and pale he looks!

Salazar. Come, father, let us take our guns at once.
This poor man's story is revolting. Come!
If you suspect the murderer near by,
We follow you, if you will lead the way.

Juarez. Thanks! Warmest thanks! I hold you to your word.
But now, I will not blight your happiness;
Forgive the speech that spread a moment's gloom,
The heart was full, and so the mouth would flow.
Now that I may rely upon your help,
Let me forget my troubles for awhile,
And try to be less sad among the gay.

Donna Arteaga. Have you been lately at the capital?
We have not heard the news for many days.

Juarez. Yes, I could tell a pretty tale from there.

Donna Arteaga. Here, eat and drink and tell us all you know.

Juarez.   Not long ago I went to Mexico,
And all the city was adorned with flags;
The Cortez council was assembled there,
To change anew the country's government.
My cousin, who was janitor up there,
Procured me easily a hiding place,
From where I saw the crazy farce, disguised;
That is—I mean—well dressed in decent clothes.

   Arteaga [*angrily*].   "A crazy farce!" The Cortez serious vote!

   Juarez [*bitterly*].   Ha! ha! Had you but seen the cruel joke!
With frowning brow, and with his doubled fist,
The Maréchal of France walked bluntly up
To every Cortez, and with rasping voice,
He said: "I take your vote (with your consent)
For Emperor Maximilian; is that right?
Of course he is your choice. Why don't you speak?"
And humbly every Cortez answered, "Yes."

   Schoolmaster.   That was the way; I saw it all myself,
For with the children I was ordered there;
One hundred soldiers joined the chorus, too.
We cried, "Hurrah!" to close with grand effect.

   Juarez.   Now, do you hear it? Come and fill a glass;
Long life to freedom and the people's rights.

   Salazar.   That is no right—not as you show it there;
The devil may respond to such a toast.

   Juarez.   What is the difference, if the end is good?
True, they still burn and murder, here and there;
But that will change, like many other things.
The lands, for instance, that were taken from

The greedy priests, and now so richly bloom,
Will be returned to monast'ry's dead hand.

Arteaga. What, all of them? Not this fine cloister farm!

Juarez. That is but little for an emp'ror's throne.

Arteaga. But then the State must pay us for the land.

Juarez. And if they gave you all their treasury
You would have nothing but a pile of debts.

Arteaga. They cannot, dare not, do such unjust acts!

Donna Mejia. Trust not the man who spreads such discontent
Who is he that you should believe his word.

Juarez [*giving him a paper*].
Look here; here is the paper. Read yourselves.

Arteaga [*reading*].
By Jove! they shall not drive me from my farm,
That I have nursed for years just like a child!

Juarez. Read on. They mean to take your children, too;
To drill and educate them by the priests
In Greek and Latin and—despotic rule.

Salazar And then, perhaps, forget their mother tongue;
Their manly liberty! What burning shame!

Juarez. 'Tis only for the sake of blessed peace;
That you shall have, though it should only be
The graveyard's dead and everlasting peace;
Let us again send forth a loud hurrah,
For Emperor and peace. What? You are dumb!
You seemed so full of joy and praise just now——

Guests. We want no peace—not such a peace as that!

O do not mention that imperial name!
Are we such fools, that they can play with us?

Donna Mejia.   Accursed man, why do you spur them on?

Juarez.   I do not spur; I cut the cataract
That seems to blind the people's mental eye.

Arteaga.   My God, how very blind we must have been!

Inez [*to mother*].
Oh! were this but a dream.   It bodes no good.

Juarez.   And do you recognize the robber now.
Who would enslave me, you, and every one?
Behold in me our freedom's champion.
Arouse yourselves and seize again your arms,
For I, old Juarez, I will lead you on!

All.   What, Juarez here? The hero in our midst?

Scene IV.

The same.   Porfirio Diaz.

Porfirio [*rushing in*].   We are surrounded by imperial troops!

Juarez.   Now then, redeem the promise that you gave;
Defend your liberty, your house and farm.

Arteaga.   I will, with all my heart.

Guests.   And I—and I;
We all will fight; come, let us get the guns!
                        [*Exit Arteaga and Guests.*

Schoolmaster.   Great science stands above the partisans.
                        [*Exit.*

Salazar. My poor, beloved wife, how short a joy!

Inez. O Salazar, don't leave me or I die.

Salazar. Compose yourself, sweet bride. When we have slain
The enemy, I will return to you.
Then we will celebrate another feast,
Uninterrupted by a despot's scheme.
        [*Tears himself away. Exit.*

Donna Arteaga [*weeping*].
My poor, dear, good old husband! 'Tis too bad!

Juarez. Good women, clear the furniture away,
And then take refuge on some neighboring farm.

Donna Arteaga. O what a scourge! The Lord be merciful!
        [*They clear the stage and exit.*

Donna Mejia. Mejia's house you shall not occupy;
His wife will not admit such rebel hordes.

Juarez [*to soldiers*]. Take her away that she may not betray——
        [*She draws a dagger.*
Yes, stab me, if you like. What counts one man?

Donna Mejia. No, not the death of martyrdom enjoy.
A traitor, you shall die by hangman's hand.
        [*Exit as prisoner.*

SCENE V.

JUAREZ, PORFIRIO, ARTEAGA, SALAZAR and Guests.

[*They come back uniformed and furnished with different weapons*].

Guests. We are prepared and wait your orders now.

Juarez [*to Arteaga and Salazar*]. What was your rank?

Arteaga. I was a major once.

Salazar. A captain, I, though not experienced
As here my father;—full of courage, too.

Juarez. Swear on this flag allegiance unto death.

All. We swear!

Juarez [*to Arteaga and Salazar*].
Now, show that you deserve my faith,
For I will trust you with a small command;
Your house and yard shall be your fortress now.
Porfirio, stay and station all the troops;
Make safe the buildings on your right and left.
I hurry to the center. Time is short.
Stand true and firm, and trust in God!

All. Hurrah!

[*Music, marching, counter-marching, firing. Mejia's troops break into the yard. Truce.*

Scene VI.

Mejia, Salazar, Arteaga, Soldiers, etc.

Mejia. Surrender in the Emp'ror's name! How now!
You, Salazar and Arteaga, you
Among these men? What has misled you so?

Arteaga [*at window*].
We are protecting freedom, house and home.

Mejia. And turn my house into a hostile fort!
O, do not force an old and trusting friend
To turn into your executioner,
By such revolting crime of treachery.

Arteaga.   Still more revolting I would call the crime
That you should be the murderer of your friends,
And, joined to foreign fiends, call down upon
Your head the curses of your native land.

Mejia.   Had you been better patriots, the throne
Would have been safe without the foreign help.

Arteaga.   Had you been better patriots, the land
Would have been safe without the foreign throne.

Mejia.   Enough of useless words.   Unbolt this door.
Will you surrender, miserable fools?

Salazar.   Stand back and save your life, or I will fire.

Mejia.
That seals your doom.   Come on, boys!   Storm the house.
          [*They storm the houses; fire breaks out.*

SCENE VII.

Mexico.   Maximilian's Palace.   Audience Room.

Max.   How different do politics appear,
Viewed from the high position of a throne,
Than from the valley of the multitudes,
Who scarcely see what is quite near at hand.
The consequences that seem clear as day,
When in due time they follow human deeds,
How difficult are they to weigh before;
And yet, it seems, I must allow the press,
That judges all I do by mere results,
To criticise this act or that reform,

Or praise a speech with faintly hidden scorn,
Half understood or mutilated quite.
They soon mislead their readers; thoughtless crowd.
Must I allow it after all? And why?
Because in weak enthusiasm once,
I dreampt to govern with a gentle hand,
And looked on liberty from lower spheres.
Short-sighted, cruel men, I used to call
My friend—my brother, too—for their strict laws,
Because I thought—O, vain imagining—
That I had found the spell in Nature's laws,
How to combine unbounded liberty
With stern, eternal order. Happy dream!
What have I gained by magnanimity?
What by the pile of generous decrees,
Composed in Miramare in advance,
In order to be signed in Mexico.
Why, nothing have I gained but what the sword
Of that untiring Maréchal of France
Has conquered. He, the mighty Emp'ror's arm,
Who, though with constant sacrifices, he
Adds to my strength, extending my domain,
Has modestly withdrawn from praise and thanks,
So that I hardly see him here at court.
No, no! This people is not ripe for laws
Such as might suit a highly cultured land.
What I so often have condemned and fought,
The censure of the press, I must adopt,
So these rebellious papers may not stir
The simple-minded people to revolt,
Until they fall as victims to my troops.

At other times they have defiled the acts
And best intentions, of my truest friends;—
It must be stopped; and that without delay,—
The freedom of the press is thus abridged. [*Signs the decree.*
I almost hesitate—well, for a while—
I must not check the marshal's valiant strength
With halting weakness, that so many times
Has undermined what had been bravely won.
I cannot stand the mild but withering
Reproaches for my hesitating acts,
That strike me with but ill-concealed contempt,
In La Bastida's smooth yet biting speech.
Come forth once more, thou blackest of decrees,
That in a bitter moment I conceived,
And then destroyed, but now again renew;
With great deliberation I must act.
For months I call this Mexico my own,
And still the war seems never ending. No!
This vile rebellion must come to an end.
[*Reads*]. "All who are found with weapons in their hands,
Resisting law and government, shall be
Court-martialed, executed on the spot,
And their estates fall to the treasury."
A cruel law; and yet there is no help.
What sacrifices one man may save ten.
That is my consolation. [*He signs*]. It is done,
And yet—I will consider—still 'tis mine.

Scene VIII.

Maximilian, Carlotta, then Lares.

Carlotta [*without*]. O, let me be the first to break the news
To my beloved lord.

Max. Speak, dearest wife;
Good news, no doubt, my guardian angel brings.

Carlotta. Rejoice! rejoice! The victory is ours.
A messenger just galloped into court.
But I persisted I would be the first
To tell the glorious tale. For I was sure
That you would clasp the first one to your breast,
And that embrace no other should enjoy.

Max. [*embracing her*].
Indeed, who would not kiss such messenger;
But where delays the man? I wish to hear.

Carlotta. He spoke to Lares. See, he's coming now.

Max. My dear, good Lares, is it true, indeed?

Lares. Yes; here are the dispatches. Praise to God!
[*He presents the dispatches.*

Max. [*reading*]. 'Tis true, by Heaven! Beaten everywhere!
Six thousand prisoners of war they took!
Among them are three gen'rals! Great Bazaine!
[*He opens another dispatch.*
And here, Mejia, fighting at the head
Of his brave Mexicans, had grand success!
That is as welcome news as any yet.
[*He opens a third dispatch.*

What! Juarez disappeared! He has perhaps
Flown from the country! O, the joyful news!
At last I am the master of my land,
And happiness and harmony return,—
Let us take hold with new encouragement.

Lares. And sternly judge all plotters of revolt.

Carlotta. Severity again, and nothing else!

Scene IX.

The same. LA BASTIDA. FATHER VISCHER. AGUIRRE. CAMPOS. Court.

La Bastida. I am rejoiced that it has pleased the Lord
To send your Majesty this great success.

Father Vischer. Your Majesty's most humble servant joins
In these congratulations with delight.

Aguirre. I can but say the same with all my heart.

Campos. O, may this victory mean lasting peace.

Max. I thank you, gentlemen, that you have come
To share with me the happiness I feel.
Here, read yourselves the news of victory.
And now let us return with energy
To those much needed government reforms.
Here are the laws that I had signed in doubt,
With confidence I place them in your hands.
You, worthy Campos, will not find it hard,
By an increase of tariff to procure
The needed means to carry out the work;
Such outlays will repay us well in time.

Campos. I will exert myself, your Majesty.
But pray do not expect too much at first;
A patient, when his fever heat subsides,
Appears much weaker than he did before;
Just so the State, when frenzied war has passed.

Max. And you, Aguirre, education's guard,
Will have a difficult position now.
The present State, whatever we may do,
Will be but patchwork at the very best.
The future State should form one solid whole,
And we should educate accordingly.
The children should not work from early youth,
In common labor that exhausts their strength.
No. Every child hereafter shall be taught
Religion first of all; philosophy,
The ancient languages and history.
For only early-drilled and well-taught minds,
Combine with freedom due respect for law.
The further details of the law are here.   [*Hands it to him.*
The parents who, in cruel selfishness,
Withhold the children from the common school,
To draw scant wages from the tiny hands,
Shall, first, be warned; and in the second case,
The children shall be taken from their care.

Aguirre. Your Majesty, it is a dangerous thing,
Such sudden change among the lower class.

Max. If dangerous at all, but for a while,
Until success convinces prejudice.
When well refined and educated youths
Return to their delighted parents' homes,

Then all will see the blessings of reform.
Compulsion will be nominal, and I
Can give my people all their freedom back;
But for the present, here the censure law. [*Gives it to Lares.*

Lares [*whispers*]. Well, that is something.

La Bastida [*whispers*]. But not quite enough!

Max. Now, gentlemen, I hope you will attend
To everything without delay.

La Bastida. May I
Make one suggestion?

Max. Honored father, speak.

La Bastida. Exalted minds, accustomed but to soar
In lighter spheres, detect the distant goal,
Where those who walk the ground see but the road;
But this, let me assure your Majesty,
We humbler men see better than yourself.
Lead us your way, and we will follow you;
But take our warning kindly when we point
To stumbling-blocks with which the road is strewn.
The censure and the school laws, good and wise,
Will yet remain half measures after all;—
They will cause opposition everywhere;
They taunt the lion, but they do not tame.
Do not suppose the rebel strength subdued
Because their fighting troops have met defeat;
In many hearts the loyalty is faint,
And treachery still rankles in the breasts
Of plotting men, behind the mask of faith;
Assassins lurk around the palace still.

Be quite the man that present times demand;
Do not shrink back from those decisive acts
That you so loudly praise in other men,
But issue the decree that you withdrew,
Crush out the last suspicion of revolt,
For only then you will rule free from care.

   Max. I knew it but too well; the same reproach!
For once, however, you have judged me wrong.
The law that you so urgently demand
I have just signed.

   Carlotta.   What! not the document
That yesterday you promised to destroy!

   Max. The same. It seems quite indispensable.
Well it is ready to be countersigned.

   Carlotta. Hold, Maximilian; do not be too quick.
When I, just now, proclaimed the joyful news,
You called me guardian angel; let me now
In warning be your guardian angel too.
Do not estrange the hearts that turn to us!
Do you remember what we promised once,
That, when the rebel hordes had been destroyed,
Sweet mercy should replace strict punishment?

   Lares. But, noble Empress, when temptation stops,
Is not the treason doubly criminal?

   Carlotta. If, as you say, temptation's voice is dead,
Will not the crime of treason disappear?

   Lares. Whene'er the crime shall cease, your Majesty.
This stringent law will be dead letter soon;

Besides, you still retain the glorious right
To pardon where blind justice would condemn.

   Carlotta. Well, then, to older wisdom I submit,
And trust that mercy may avert the worst.

   Max. So let it be. You, gentlemen, will see
That all these laws are promptly carried out;
[*to Major Domo*] And for to-night I want the grandest feast
That ever these old castle walls have seen,
To celebrate the day with joy and pomp.
Invite all loyal grandees of my realm;
Be sure to bid Prince Iturbide come,
The Princess likewise, his most noble aunt;
Proclaim the victory throughout the land,
And on the plazza make a barbecue;
Set out a hundred casks of beer and wine,
So that the people may rejoice with us.
[*To Ministers.*] I hope to see you all at court to-night.
                [*Exit with Carlotta and Court.*

   La Bastida [*to Father Vischer*].
And so at last we have achieved success.
Fail not to put in force, with utmost speed,
This bloody law that will avenge the church
For many insults and the loss of lands.

   Father Vischer.
No fear, your reverence; you know my zeal.

   La Bastida [*to the others*].
The Lord be with you, friends, and lead you right.

   Lares. And may he bless your noble work! Good night.
                [*Exit all but Father Vischer.*

Scene X.

FATHER VISCHER. Later, INEZ and DONNA ARTEAGA.

Father Vischer. Yes; I declare I love our mother church.
What was my lot before she took me up?
A scholar first; then teacher, smuggler, spy,
Gold digger in the West—from bad to worse;
Now that I'm "Father" I am everything,
And swing—the right hand of my Emperor—
The cudgel over many thousand heads.

Servant. Two women from the country stand outside;
They bring petitions to the Emperor.

Father Vischer. Two pretty women? And without a man?
Let them come in. [*Enter Donna Arteaga and Inez.*
Approach, good women. [*Aside.*] Oh!
The one is old and ugly! [*Aloud.*] Pretty maid,
Come, tell me freely what is your desire.

Inez. My husband and my father are confined——

Father Vischer [*aside, softly*].
Her husband! Hm! So she is married, too!

Donna Arteaga.
They always have been loyal to the crown,
But were seduced with smooth and glittering words.

Father Vischer. Aha! I understand. They broke the law;
In prison now; and will be soon piff, paff!

Donna Arteaga.
They won't be shot! The Lord have mercy! No!

Father Vischer.
Don't scream like that at Court.   Look here, old dame,
Go into yonder room, and from that door
You soon will see the Emperor appear.
So keep a good look out; don't miss your chance,
While your good daughter will explain the case.

Donna Arteaga.
Yes, yes.   God grant that we are not too late!   [*Exit.*

Father Vischer.   Now, listen, my good girl, and do not cry.
Do you behold that paper on the desk?
While that is mine, your husband's life is safe;
But when the law contained in that decree
Has left my hands, the men you love must die.

Inez [*kneeling*].   O, then, retain the paper in your hands
Till we invoke the monarch's mercy, pray!

Father Vischer [*aside*].   How beautiful she is!   Adorable!
[*Aloud.*]   Arise, my poor, my dear, my lovely maid,—
No; woman, I would say,—all shall be done
That in my power lies; for, queer to say,
The very moment that I saw your face
My heart was yours in pity and in love.

Inez.   Then let us hurry to his Majesty!

Father Vischer.
No, child.   At court things do not move so fast;
Besides, my orders are: "without delay"
To have that miserable law proclaimed;
And strictly punished is all negligence;
And yet for such a dear and darling wench——

Inez.   No!   Let me go!   O, why this long delay?

Father Vischer. Come, follow me in yonder little room,
And tell me all about your troubles there.
Perhaps I can console with fervent prayer,
And as we learn to know each other well,
In cosy friendship, I might take my chance,
And put my duties off a little while.

Inez. Why in that little room? Why not right here?
And don't you know enough about my grief?
[*Aside*]. He stares at me as if he meant no good!
[*Aloud*]. No, no! I will not follow you in there.

Father Vischer [*aside*].
She seems at last to comprehend my scheme.
[*Aloud*]. You foolish girl, why do you hesitate?
Two ways, I tell you, only go from here:
The one leads into that boudoir with you;
The other, to the prison with that law.

Inez. What shall I do! [*Clasping her hands in despair.*

Father Vischer. No affectation; come,
Is not my kindness worth a fair reward?

Inez. You miserable man, if it be true,
That in your hands you hold my husband's life,
Far better he should die through his own deed,
Than live dishonored by my infamy.

Father Vischer. Must I compel you then to your own good!
[*He takes hold of her.*

Inez. Stand back from me! Help! Mother!

Scene XI.

The same. Donna Arteaga and Dr. Basch hurry in from opposite sides.

Donna Arteaga. What goes on?

Dr. Basch. Who calls?

Father Vischer. Be silent, or your husband dies!

Inez. I thought—I felt—I was about to faint.

Donna Arteaga [*to Doctor*].
O, worthy sir, let me entreat your help;
Procure an audience with his Majesty,
That we may plead for our poor husbands' lives.

Dr. Basch. Why, certainly I will, come! Follow me
As soon as possible.

Donna Arteaga. The Lord be blessed!
   [*Dr. Basch threatens Father Vischer with his finger.
   Exit with the women.*

Father Vischer. Yes, shake your finger, you old Philis'ine!
Though I am forced to let the damsel slip,
I hold the husband in my deadly grip.   [*Exit with the decree.*

Scene XII.

Banquet Hall.

Maximilian, Carlotta, La Bastida, Father Vischer, Mejia, Prince and Princess Iturbide and Court.

Max.
Sound trumpets! Drums roll forth your thundering voice!

Proclaim to all the great victorious day,
That after all the sufferings of war,
Brings back to us prosperity and peace.
Be welcome, brave Mejia, at my court;
How glad I am that you could leave the troops,
In order to receive from my own hands
This decoration for your valiant deeds.

       [Gives him the decoration.

 Mejia. My sovereign, you make me feel ashamed.
I only did my duty. Heaven knows
How hard it was at Sierra Gorda.

 Max.   No!
All Mexico owes you a debt of thanks.
The present needs no more our constant watch,
And we can look into the future now,
With courage and with greater confidence.
Let us to-day a crowning keystone lay
To Hapsburg's house—cemented as it was
With our best citizens' most precious blood—
That it may stand unshaken by the storms.
It has not pleased the Lord to bless us with
An heir to follow us upon the throne.
We, therefore, have resolved—in order that
Succession may not breed fraternal war—
To choose the next successor to the crown,
In everything exactly like my son.
And who could seem more worthy of that place
Than he whose great imperial ancestor
Has died a martyr for this country's weal.
Prince Iturbide, come into my arms,

You are henceforth the crown prince of the realm;
Receive a blessing from your father's hand.

Carlotta. And all the love that I once vainly hoped
I might bestow on children of my own,
Shall now be heaped upon your blessed head.

Prince Iturbide. May heaven long preserve such parents' life,
That head and heart be trained by their advice
Before I shall be called to rule this land.

Max. Dear princess, be a faithful sister hence.

Princess Iturbide. I cannot well express my thanks in words,
My honored prince—beloved brother now—
But to your welfare, and my nephew's here,
I will, from this day forth, devote my life.

All. Long live the Emperor! Long live the Prince!
[*Blast of trumpets, etc.*

Scene XIII.

The same. Donna Arteaga. Donna Inez. Dr. Basch.

Donna Arteaga. Have mercy! Pardon!

Inez. Help! your Majesty!

Max. Who let you in? And what does all this mean?

Dr. Basch. My Emperor, forgive this act of mine;
I was unable to restrain their zeal,
They are the wives of hostile generals,
Named Arteaga, Sire; and Salazar,

Who have been taken prisoners of war,
And with some others are condemned to death.

 Max. How now! Without my knowledge or consent.

 Father Vischer.
"Court-martialed on the spot," says the decree.

 Carlotta. No, Max; on such a day no blood should flow.
Now is the time; be great and merciful.

 Dr. Basch. Sire, do not let these women beg in vain.

 Max. With pleasure I concede your ardent wish;
No executions on a day like this.
Make out a pardon; I will sign it now.

 Inez. O, mother, mother, all is well again!
The sudden change quite overpowers me,
Despair and happiness so closely knit.

 Max. [*writing*]. You, Father Vischer, messenger of death,
Shall be the herald of my pardon now.
Make haste, that you may reach the men in time.

 La Bastida [*aside to Father Vischer*].
I hope you understand what time *I* mean.

 Father Vischer. Your Excellency, I do.

 Max.   Here, hurry off!
   [*Exit Father Vischer with pardon.*

 Donna Arteaga. Your Majesty, my language is too weak
To thank you for——

 Max.   Nay, my good woman, go,
And be as happy as I am myself.

Carlotta.   My glorious dreams are now reality;
Might, right and mercy are combined in you.

Max.   Come on, my friends, to feast, and to be gay,
And celebrate with me my happiest day.

END OF SECOND ACT.

ACT III.

Scene I.

Camp. On the left, at a table, Austrians and Belgians; on the right, Frenchmen.

1st Austrian.
Come, drink, good friends, a toast to war and camp;
A man can show his worth on battle fields,
Where not mere favors will promote to rank,
But strength and courage make a soldier's way.
To-day, we win and whip the enemy;
To-morrow, they whip us. A jolly life!

2d Austrian. That shows the man from wild Bohemia.
Had you been born a Viennese, like me,
You would adopt the higher view of war.
We seek not fighting, but what fighting brings;
The motto, "Right and Emp'ror,"—that is grand!

1st Belgian. I cannot see that "Right" they talk about.
I wish I were in Belgium, and in peace;
The devil take the whole wild-goose chase here!

1st Austrian. You call yourselves good soldiers?

2d Belgian. No, we don't.
We were enticed with glorious promises
To settle in this land, with wife and child,

Armed, it is true. for our protection's sake,
But not to hunt a distant enemy,
And march and starve with neither rest nor pay.

3d Austrian.   Such men as you disgrace our regiment.
Had not those men been always pushed ahead,
We should have had the glory to ourselves.

1st Frenchman.
Do you mean us?   You soon can have it all,
For we will not much longer be the fools
To do your Emp'ror's work without reward.
Be not too sure that we will not be missed,
And that you will not long for our brave troops
When Juarez is pursuing at your heels.

2d Austrian.   Go when you will; for, had you never come,
The revolution would have long been stopped,
While you are constantly reviving it
By murd'rous pillaging——

2d Frenchman.   Parbleu! you fool!
We murderers?   What does your government?
It butchers all the prisoners of war.

2d Austrian.
That is not true; they have been pardoned all.

2d Frenchman.   Yes; pardoned after it was just too late.

1st Belgian.   I fear the clergy is to blame for that.

1st Austrian.   Cursed heretic!   You dare insult the priests.

1st Frenchman.
The pris'ners' funeral procession!   Look!—
They say Porfirio Diaz was reprieved.

Scene II.

The same. Funeral procession, followed by a crowd.

Donna Arteaga and Inez.

Donna Arteaga. Be proud, great soldiers of an Emperor!
See here the work that you have helped to do.
Is this the way you give your country peace?
Eternal peace you give us; that is true.

2d Austrian.
Say, woman, you had better hold your tongue;
You have most generously been allowed
A formal funeral. Are these your thanks?
Do not arouse bad blood, but go your way.

Donna Arteaga. To laud the Emperor is treachery?
Wherever I may go, his praise shall sound.
How smooth his speech! How merciful his words!
And, if a bloody deed then follows them,
It surely is a mere mistake—a slight
Misunderstanding by the underlings.
Be proud, you soldiers of an Emperor!
I wish you joy of such heroic deeds!

2d Frenchman. You see, your Emperor did murder them.

2d Austrian.
How dare you use such language, you French dog!
Quick! swallow that, or I will choke it down. [*Draws.*

1st Frenchman. Stand back, *canaille!* [*Draws.*

1st Austrian. Draw! Knock those beggars down!
[*Hand to hand fight. Exit.*

Donna Arteaga.
Now do your work—hate, jealousy and spite,—
And open wide a road for just revenge
To claim atonement for this bloody crime.
                    [*Turning toward the body*
And you who failed in life, though true and strong,
In death you will revenge your people's wrong!

Scene III.

Palace Garden at Mexico.

Porfirio Diaz.

Porfirio Diaz.   I wish I could enjoy this lovely day,
As in my early childhood's home,—and yet,
How full of hardships has my freedom been;
How rich in comforts is my prison house.
Perhaps it would have been the best for me,
To have been shot, together with my friends,
Before the monarch's mercy saved my life,
And now he treats me better than a friend.
My word, my oath compel me hence to fly;
My heart and mind are held in friendship's bonds.
What shall I do?   Where can I find advice?
For ever gone is all my hope in life.
Who would have thought a Diaz thus could sway
Between his duty and his heart's desire.
If for this Emperor I draw my sword,
I am a traitor to my people.   Fie!
Shall I then waste my time in idleness?

Or shall I fly from here to join my troops,
And help to crush this man, my truest friend?
And will I serve my people after all,
If I, with uncouth hordes, destroy a prince
Who, with exalted mind, rules strong and well,
And certainly with no more tyranny
Than Juarez, freedom's stern defender, does?
But who is to succeed the Emperor?
And who will follow then? Not on the vote
Of those that will be ruled does that depend.
No, only on the accident of birth;
Although the Emp'ror says: "The Grace of God!"
Oh! if he would shake off the ties of birth,
Be satisfied to be like other men,
He still would rule by his superior mind;
Would captivate all others like myself.
And Princess Iturbide—— Bah! No use!

Scene IV.

Porfirio Diaz. Maximilian. Later, Carlotta and Princess Iturbide.

Max. Porfirio, sad again, and all alone?
What weighs on you; is it imprisonment?
Is it the death of friends that bows you down?—
Although I gladly would have saved their lives.
The punishment was not unmerited.

Porfirio. And did not I, like all those others, swear
To never rest until you had been destroyed?

Max. Think not of that; that problem will be solved;
Have but a little patience. Ah! behold!
The ladies come.   [*Enter Carlotta and Princess Iturbide.*
                 You have arrived in time
To help disperse the whims of our young friend;
Smooth down the wrinkles on his frowning brow;
I know you can, the Princess best of all.
And now that here and there a threatening cloud
Seems to obscure the sky of politics,
And unexpected hindrances increase
The difficulties of my daily work,
I more than ever need a smiling face;
Let me soon find you in a cheerful mood,
So that I may forget the cares and plaints
And all the trouble of the council room.

   Carlotta. What is the matter, Max? You seem oppressed.
                 [*Exit Maximilian and Carlotta.*

Scene V.

PORFIRIO DIAZ and PRINCESS ITURBIDE.

   Porfirio. Fair Princess——

   Princess.   General!

   Porfirio.   You seem to be
Of serious mind; in fact for many days
I have observed your color fade away.
You do not suffer?

   Princess.   No;—and yet, like you.
We both grew up among the balmy woods,

And cannot thrive here in the hot-house air.
Wild plants will never prosper when confined,
Though nursed and fostered with the greatest care,
The leaves hang wilting and the blossoms fall;
They need the forest's peace and solitude.

Porfirio.   You talk like that, though you are not in bonds?

Princess.
Who knows; perhaps more firmly bound than you—
But no; away with all these gloomy thoughts.
Tell me again about your mountain home;
Of farm, and house, and of those laughing eyes
That archly peeped through neighbor's hawthorn hedge
Across the lawn to where the youngster sat,
Who afterwards became a general.
That always makes you smile, and cheers me up.

Porfirio.   Those thoughts of home now also make me sad.
My poor old father, how he used to tell
Of vile intrigues and lies at royal courts;
How he would boast of free republics' rights.
I listened, with enthusiastic glow—
I loved and hated thoroughly; and now?
I am no more the boy I was, no more
The fiery hater of all royalty;
For I have seen too much, to follow out,
One-sidedly, the blind instincts of man,
That might have led me to a righteous end;
Too little, to feel sure of what is right,—
And doubts are thus revolving in my mind.

Princess.   I wish I could assist——

Porfirio.   Perhaps you can.
As through the thorny, wildly tangled hedge
Of olden times, so now, I see again,
Through all the puzzling labyrinth of doubt,
Two eyes of sparkling black, more beautiful
Than all the eyes I ever saw before;
Two eyes that would dispel all cares and doubt.
Those eyes, adored Princess, they are yours.
   Princess.   O, General!
   Porfirio.   Nay, your devoted slave,
And at your feet I pledge to you my love;
For, since those eyes have beamed into my heart,
I prize this golden cage so very high
That even if the door stood wide ajar
I could not fly away from where you are.
   Princess.   And yet you swore to stand by Juarez' cause,
And fight till Emp'ror Max should be subdued.
   Porfirio.   Say, fairest, that you will control my deeds;
Your word shall be my oracle in all.
If to obey the Emp'ror you command,
I hold myself from other pledges free,
Absolved from all my sins through purest love.
O, speak!
   Princess.   Not here and now, my friend.   I think
I hear a footstep on the path near by.
Quick, General; arise.   If we were seen———.
   Porfirio.   But when will you decide my pending fate?
When may I have a word with you alone?
   Princess.   Well, let me see.   Come late to my boudoir;

Perhaps I then will give my new-made slave
A difficult commission to perform.

 Porfirio.   I will be there.   But, stay;—how can I come?
The spies, that La Bastida sends to watch,
Patrol about the palace gates at night.
He does not trust me as the Emp'ror does.

 Princess.   Yes, yes, I know,—he watches everything;
But with this key, that fits the inside gate,
You can reach, unobserved, the other wing.
And now, good-by. I pray you stay no more—
Until to-night, my wild, romantic friend.

 Porfirio.   Until to-night, my much beloved queen.   [*Exit.*

 Princess.   How happy he departs, my poor young friend;
Just like all men—for they are all alike.
They think they rule the world,—us women, too,—
While many times they are obeying us.
A sigh, a smile, perhaps—a *negligeé*,
And out of balance goes philosophy,—
The scholar's long-trained logic yields to love.
I hardly try to win this man, and lo!
The fiery Mexican is at my feet.
O, how much safer do I hold him now
Than La Bastida's spies, who rather tend
To make him feel and hate his prison more,
Than to prevent so bold a man as he
From breaking out, if he should want to fly.
He thinks the key that I have given him
Will open him my loving heart. O, no!
It locks him faster to my Emp'ror's throne—
To him who far surpasses every one;

And how much grander, mightier could he be
Did not that weak and vacillating wife
Stand by his side to check and weaken him,
When strength and resoluteness ought to rule.
Yes; through her foolish influence alone
The almost crushed rebellion rises new.
If mine had been the fate that she enjoys,
How I could follow in his genial flight,
Could urge him when he doubts, or spur him on,
And from his head the crown would not pass on—
Perhaps—not to another woman's son.
Is not the Padre right? Were it not best
For him, for her, and for the government,
If from the Emp'ror she should separate,
Retire from court; still better, leave the land?
So that while she, from all her cares relieved,
Could strengthen her weak nerves in distant climes,
The Emperor could rule with iron hand.
Yes she must go; but how to find a way?
How can I cut the tie of clinging love
With which she has attached herself to him?
How can I mold her unsuspecting mind
To suit my plan, without creating fear,
Or possibly suspicion?— Will that do?—

SCENE VI.

CARLOTTA and PRINCESS ITURBIDE.

Carlotta. Where is the General? I thought him here,
Well taken care of in your company.

Princess. Porfirio Diaz went some time ago,
But not as sad as he appeared at first.
I cheered him up with lively pleasantries,—
Though it is difficult to joke, and smile,
And frolic, in these hard and serious times.

Carlotta. But, Princess, are the times so very hard?
I thought the worst had long been overcome,
And better days were now in store for us.

Princess. Yes; so thought I. We all have had that hope;
But, if what Father Vischer says is true,
The bitter dregs of care have not been drained.

Carlotta.
You frighten me, dear friend. What has occurred?

Princess. O, nothing positive,—but many things.
The best intentions show the worst results;
The certainty of peace grows daily less;
The troops of France seem slowly to retreat,
And close upon their heels the rebels come.
Did you not see the Emp'ror's troubled mien?

Carlotta. Yes; that he often was in bitter mood
I noticed; but I did not think it was
The burden of the cares of government.
He spoke of Miramare with regrets,
And, evidently from a kind regard,
He tried to hide from me his many cares,
That I might rest in peace.

Princess. I have no doubt!

Carlotta. O, how much more contented I would be
If he confided all these cares to me;

I would console him, and inspire new hope.
Why cannot women help a little more?

 Princess. They help still less, I fear, than they might do.

 Carlotta. What do you mean? Could you suggest a way
To make myself more useful in this world;
With pleasure I would seize the chance.

 Princess.   Perhaps!

 Carlotta. O, speak, dear Princess, for I long to hear!

 Princess. You see, what on a smaller scale we call
Society, upon a larger scale,
Among the nations, we call politics;
Just as the families associate,—
And every one would like to be the first,—
So do the states contend for wealth and might:
As we have quarrels, they declare a war;
A wedding, here, is called a treaty, there,—
Both tied forever, yet so apt to break;
Our school for scandal, is their public press,
Discussing everything, without much truth.
Now, tell me, is it not the woman's place
To manage house and home, and smartly judge
One neighbor's weakness, and the other's worth:
We knit the lover's knot; we manage men;
And, in a word, we lead society.

 Carlotta. Of course!

 Princess.   And have we not, in politics,
The self-same people, with the same weak points?
Why should we not be fit to manage them?
I do believe, your Majesty, we could

Be better diplomats than many men,
If we but had the confidence to try.

 Carlotta. Indeed, how often I have thought of that
Which you set forth in clear, convincing words;
And yet, how can we women understand
The schemes and rank intrigues of diplomats?

 Princess. An untrained statesman may succeed, at times,
By ready wit, where long-schooled wisdom fails.
How many diplomats have had the chance
To gather an experience such as ours?
The tender bud of your sweet, child-like mind,
Has suddenly developed to a flower
Of ripe experience and of serious thought;
The child has grown to be a woman now,
All in a short but most eventful time.
Are you resolved to serve your noble spouse,
And to relieve him of his heavy load
Of serious cares? Then ask him, nay, entreat,
To let you have a share in state affairs.

 Carlotta. With every hour I feel more confidence;
Thanks, dearest friend, for your most kind advice;
Of course, he ought to share with me his cares,
As once, in by-gone times, we shared all joys.
I hurry to him, open up my heart,
And offer him my faithful services;
He smiles, astonished,—gently shakes his head;
Then I must shrewdly overcome his doubts,
Till he consents,—a victim of the first
Example of my diplomatic skill;
And, once convinced, he will confide in me;

His love will strengthen me where I am weak,
And carry me along till I succeed.   [*Exit*.

Princess.   Perhaps it carries you to distant shore;
Good luck, Carlotta, if we meet no more.

Scene VII.

Audience Room.

Maximilian.   Bazaine.

Max.   Be welcome, Maréchal; I am much pleased
To see you here, at court, at last.

Bazaine.   I bring,
Your Majesty, my dutiful respects,
And I have come, according to your wish,
As soon as war and service would permit.

Max.   For all past service take my hearty thanks;
But with more pleasant feelings I would have
Received you as victorious general,
Than now, as leader of retreating troops.
Where is the courage that the Frenchman boasts?
Is it our neigbour's threats that caused your fight?

Bazaine.   Retreat, your Majesty, is not a flight!
The troops have not lost courage, nor have I;
It is a soldier's duty to obey:
I did not ask for any reasons, Sire,
But followed out the orders I received.

Max.   How can that be?   I do not recollect
That I have given orders to retreat.

Bazaine.   I had the orders from *my* Emperor ;
I am a Frenchman.

   Max. [*aside*].   Ah!

   Bazaine.   But no command,
I knew, would come from France, unless the same
Had been approved of by your Majesty;
And when two monarchs are so closely joined
By friendship and by interest alike,
There, to obey the one, can only mean
To serve the other.

   Max. [*aside*].   Can he really mean
To play a treach'rous game?   It cannot be!
[*Aloud.*]   How far have you concluded to retreat?

   Bazaine.   Unless some counter order reaches me,
The troops will concentrate upon the coast;
Thence, be embarked to France without delay,—
As I suppose your Majesty must know.

   Max.   Yes, I remember now.   [*Aside.*]   How can it be!

   Bazaine.   The Miramare treaty is fulfilled,
By which the troops of France were to remain,
In Mexico, no longer than required,
To form an army of this nation's men,
In numbers and equipment well prepared
To guard the land.

   Max.   So reads the treaty: yes,—
But it is easier to form the troops
On paper than it is in flesh and blood.
The time, it seems to me, has not arrived
When I can quite rely upon these troops,

And, therefore, I desire you, Maréchal,
To change your plans, and to advance again;
At any rate, to hold your present points
Until I further correspond with France.

   Bazaine. I would be pleased to follow your command,
Without a moment's hesitation, Sire;
As long, however, as my orders read
To move my army to the eastern coast,
And as my troops are still without their pay,—
Without the promised ammunition, too;
As long as in this land, instead of thanks,
We reap but envy and base calumny;
And, till the wishes of your Majesty
Are fully in accord with those of France,
You must permit me strictly to obey
The stringent orders of my Emperor.

   Max. Ah! now I see you are no general—
A common tool! Go, blindly to obey
The blindly given orders, while you may.   [*Exit Bazaine.*

Scene VIII.

Maximilian. Later, La Bastida.

   Max. Conceited leader of those mighty troops,
You think to play me false behind my back;
Such low deceit was never planned in France!
I will despatch a message to my friend,
And ask him to recall this impudent
And faithless man;—and yet, dared he talk thus,

Did he not know the Emperor's intent?
The servant but reflects his master's mind.
Can it be possible?   A Bonaparte!
Undaunted as he stands before the world,
Dares not resist the threats from Washington.
He may not be the true, unselfish friend,
The great philanthropist, he seemed to me:
That sorrowful suspicion will return,
With ever growing strength, to haunt my brain.
Whatever happens, I must be prepared;
I must reorganize this nation's troops,
Provide more money—more, and more again.   [*Rings the bell.*]
Where is the Bishop?   [*to Father Vischer.*

   Father Vischer.   Still in waiting, Sire.
   Max.

Then call him.   [*Enter La Bastida.*]   Worthy father, I approach
Once more, in quest of aid, our mother church:
Will she again assist me, as before,
With means and with advice, enabling me
To carry out the great unfinished work?

   La Bastida.

The church assists those who assist the church:
When has your Majesty assisted us?
She gives advice to those who follow it:
Your Majesty would never take advice.
Have we obtained the rights to which we are
Entitled, and the confiscated lands,
That you, so long, have promised to return?
And did the government lend willing ear
To counsel and petitions from the church,

To crush, with fearless hand, the heretics,
Who grow more impudent with every day?
Are not the Jews and Protestants as good
As Catholics, to-day, in Mexico?
They hear it with astonished grief in Rome,
Where they so firmly counted on this throne.

Max. I know, good father, you have never been
In full accord with me in state affairs;
Yet, I am not as guilty as you think:
The church lands will be soon returned to you,
Though not at present; they must not be wrenched
From those who farm them now; that would create
An army of new enemies at once;
And to indemnify we have no means.
I am as good a Catholic as you,
And serve our holy church with all my heart;
But all religions seem to come from God;
As from the star of truth light radiates,
In all directions and in thousand rays,
So thousand roads lead to religious truth;
On all of them are people struggling on;
Each wand'rer sees the distant goal ahead,
And thinks his road the true and only one.
When Jews become the followers of Christ;
When Protestants adopt the Roman faith;
Both stray away from their accustomed paths,
And slowly grope their way through unknown fields.
No; let each man keep on his own straight road:
As they approach perfection, more and more,
The roads draw near to one another, too,

Until from here and there we recognize
And fully understand each other soon;
Then, hand in hand, at last, in fond embrace,
All, re-united in one faith, will march
Into the gates of Paradise regained.

  La Bastida.
Such words! And in your mouth, your Majesty!
And to such principles we should give aid!
O pray, draw back from such a precipice!
One road alone leads to eternity,
But thousands lead to the infernal gates:
Who is not with us is against us, Sire.

  Max. It seems your road and mine are not the same;
Well, follow yours, and let me go my own!
Perhaps some future day the two will meet.

  La Bastida.
Yes, may it please the Lord! But till you turn
Back from the road to everlasting sin,
And seek the church, an humble penitent,
Do not expect advice or aid from us.
O, how this news will grieve the holy Pope!   [*Exit.*

Scene IX.

  Maximilian. Later, Lares, Campos and Aguirre.

  Max. Another hope is gone. Well, well, I can
No longer feign and creep before this man;
Proud tyrant of the church, he may retain
His money, and discredit me at Rome.

O, could I cross the sea but for one hour,
See face to face my great imperial friend,
And plead my cause before the Pope in Rome,
I could regain their confidence; while now,
False statements are misrepresenting me. [*Rings.*]
[*To Father Vischer.*] Ask Lares, Campos, and the Ministers
Who may be still in waiting, to come in. [*Exit Father Vischer.*]
I must strain every nerve to save the crown. [*Enter Ministers.*]
The time is fast approaching, gentlemen,
When we, dispensing with all foreign help,
Must trust exclusively to our own strength:
Above all, Campos, find the needed funds;
I feel as if I were bound hand and foot!
Procure more means.

   Campos. The treasury is bare,
The debt is heavy, and the people poor.
We cannot trust to our resources now;
We must depend on France, or else on Rome.

   Max. From France we can expect no further help
As long as we are backward with the pay;
Besides, their troops will soon embark for home.

   Ministers. How? Is it possible; they surely go?

   Max. And Rome—the Bishop left with angry threats
Because the Church's lands were not returned;
And I am tired of all his haughty ways.

   Campos. Then I give up all hope, and must retire;
The office that I undertook with fear
And carried on with cares, I now resign
With sorrow into your imperial hands.

Max.   And with regret I take the office back.

Aguirre.   Of course, without the blessings of the church,
No other education can succeed.
Your Majesty will graciously permit
That I return to Rome.

Max. Go where you like!
There are still others. [*To Father Vischer.*] What is that you
   bring?

Father Vischer.   Here is the copy of a telegram,
From Washington, to Count of Montholon.
[*Gives it to Maximilian.*

Max. [*reading*].   It threatens serious consequences soon,
Unless the troops of France at once depart.
[*Aside.*] So, then, my first impression was correct!

Lares.   O, Sire, when all these gentlemen retire,
I cannot form another cabinet.
Put in my place another, stronger, man,
To form a better group of ministers.

Max.   Go, all of you; great men, in prosperous times,
But miserable cowards in distress;
And if in all this land there is no man
With head and heart to fill your offices,
I will hold out, fight to the bitter end,
And lead my troops to victory or death.
If I but had a messenger to France
Whom I could trust with utmost confidence!
I cannot stir from my important post,
And written words are dead; they lack the force
Of human voice, the pleading of the eye.

I think and muse, but cannot find the man;
Am I, indeed, already so forlorn?
Is there, in all this empire, far and wide,
Not one who understands me thoroughly?
Not one I can implicitly believe?

Scene X.

The same. CARLOTTA and FATHER VISCHER.

Carlotta. O, yes, dear Max, you still have such a friend,
In whom, without reserve, you may confide;
How is it that you never thought of him?

Max. Why, you surprise me! Speak, who is this friend?

Carlotta. One of the gentler sex; it is your wife.

Max. My darling child, I often think of you
In these depressing days; and, every time,
Your image has consoled and brightened me;
But, now, I need a diplomatic friend,
A trusted messenger in politics.

Carlotta. And just that place it is I come to ask;
For not alone a husband's loving wife,
An Emp'ror's worthy consort I would be.
I am no more the inexperienced child
That I was once, not many months ago;
No, at your side I learned so many things,
I formed my own opinions, heard, and saw;
For many days, I had the wish to be
Of greater service, but I feared to speak.

I am encouraged now, and full of hope;
O, trust in me, as I trust in myself!

Max. I am astonished! This determined tone—
Is it my gentle wife who speaks like this?
How could you go on such an embassy?
It takes much training and experienced skill,
A ready wit, combined with cautious tongue.

Carlotta. The honest, open way will serve us best;
And, think of it, I know my mission's aim
Before you have discussed with me your plans:
You want to reconcile his Holiness,
And keep upon such friendly terms with France
That they will further help with means and troops.

Max. Yes; you are right.

Carlotta. Well, who can bring about
This reconciliation like a wife?

Max. You tempt me almost to concede your wish.

Carlotta. What so persuasive as a woman's tongue?
And who would strive with greater zeal than I
To carry out the mission to success?

Max. I am convinced, my great, my glorious wife!
How little did I know you heretofore;
I should be grateful that an adverse fate
Has shown you in such brilliant light to me.
You are by far the worthiest of all;
No other shall be my embassador,
Although your absence will be hard to bear.
Go, gentlemen, you are no more retained,
For more than I have lost I have regained.

Scene XI.

Boudoir of Princess Iturbide.

Princess Iturbide. Then, Father Vischer.

Princess. He comes! How now? Why, Father, is it you?

Father Vischer. Do I intrude?

Princess. O, no! What secret scheme,
What pressing business, brings you here so late?

Father Vischer. Carlotta goes to France.

Princess. What; can it be?

Father Vischer. This very night, with utmost secrecy.
You laid the plan with your accustomed skill;
The whole affair appeared most natural.
Well, she once gone, we have him in our hands;
However, there is something else to do.

Princess. What else?

Father Vischer. Porfirio!

Princess. I hold him safe.

Father Vischer. H'm! do not be so very sure of that;
Although, indeed, if he could see you now,
In this most lovely, dreamy deshabile,—
That almost is enough to tempt a priest——

Princess. There—never mind; the church does not expect
Such ardent zeal.

Father Vischer. Well, well; I mean to say
He would be quite enchanted, like myself;

But yet, with nature's readily inflamed,
Reaction often follows very soon,
And what this morning he so hotly swore,
He may regret before another day;
So when he comes to-night——

 Princess.   You seem to know!

 Father Vischer. That brought me here.

 Princess.   You spy! What shall I do?
        [*Porfirio appears at the door.*

 Father Vischer. You ought to forge the iron while it's hot.
What is the use of wasting many words?
You have bewitched him with your dazzling charms;
A few more woman's tricks, a little wine,
Some dallying and ogling, and so on;
Until his brains are crazed with wine and love;—
Then, I surprise you—quick—a kiss—a ring,—
And I will bless the matrimonial bonds.

 Princess. No! no! That cannot be! Speak not like that!
I have gone far enough and risked my name
To fetter Diaz to the Emp'ror's throne.
I will not bind my heart, my life, to him,
Whose sudden wooing fills me with contempt
More than with love. No! That I cannot do!
Not for the church; nor for the government.
And, oh! not for the Emperor himself!
Until you find some other better means,
You might as well keep your advice.   [*Exit.*

 Father Vischer.   I say! [*Hurries after her.*

Scene XII.

Porfirio Diaz.

Porfirio.   Is this a dream?   Is it reality?
If true, why did I not destroy that brute
In priestly garments; and that demon, too,
Who lured me on by her angelic guise!
And yet, I am awake; this is her room;
There's where she spoke those cruel, fiendish words
That staggered me until I almost swooned!
Contempt, where I expected love for love!
With vile deceit you meant to fetter me;
False traitoress, you know not what it means
To trifle lightly with a Diaz's heart.
'Twas Providence that led me here in time
To hear you two divulge your filthy schemes:
How true, O, father, were your warning words!
This princely court seems suddenly, to me,
A vicious net of lies, and of deceit.
Can such a rotten hull contain sound fruit?
Shall I continue my research, to find
My father's words more thoroughly fulfilled,
The Emp'ror a deceiver, like the rest?
Why not?   I would not be at all surprised;
My faith in truth and purity is gone;
A horror seizes me for all of you.
Away, away from these accursed halls;
The very walls oppress and stifle me.
This key, that was to fasten me in chains,

It shall unlock the gates of freedom now.
One bitter lesson I shall take from here;
False woman's love, I tear thee from my heart!
My life shall be devoted to my work;
Away to my old flag with heart and soul,
"Destruction" shall be henceforth my parole!

Scene XIII.

Maximilian. Carlotta.

Carlotta. The storm is howling! What a fearful night!
And nearer draws the cruel parting hour,—
The hour in which we want to say so much,
Yet find so little in our grief to say.

Max. With you, my guardian angel flies away,
And leaves me to a dark, uncertain fate;
I feel as if I should not part from you—
As if I ought to sail with you for home;
There, where on lovely Miramare's shore
The waves of Adria so gently roll,
Up in the forest, where you meant to build
The little villa—do you recollect?
There we could sit, in cosy twilight's hour,
And think of by-gone times, as of weird dreams.

Carlotta. The Virgin's promise is not yet fulfilled;
The "mighty realm" is sure to be your own.

Max.
Yes; you are right; those words will yet come true;

They give me back my strength and confidence,
And drive away those dark presentiments.

Father Vischer.
Your pardon, Sire. The major urges haste:
Unless the start is made before the dawn,
He cannot guarantee a safe escape.

Max. Then it must be; good-by my darling wife!

Carlotta. Hold out; be strong until we meet again!

Max. "Until we meet again;" how long, how long,
That sounds to me!

Carlotta. Farewell! [*Exit.*

Max. Farewell! Farewell!

END OF THIRD ACT.

ACT IV.

Scene I.

Camp in Mejia's Valley. The same houses as in the First Scene of the Second Act, only somewhat demolished.

MAXIMILIAN. DR. BASCH. FATHER VISCHER.

Basch. How did you pass the night? How do you feel?

Max. Bad, Doctor, bad; how can a man repose
Beneath a roof that he has helped destroy?

Basch. Who knows; perhaps it would have been the best
If we had followed Castelnau's advice,
And joined the French when they embarked for home.

Father Vischer. Obey that haughty messenger? Indeed!

Max. Am I a puppet in the hands of France?
Go where she says? Come back when I am called?
Should I, who gave up happiness and home
For crown and fame, now cowardly retreat,
And leave this country in chaotic state?
No; no; I stay, in spite of French advice;
My presence only can save Mexico.
How now? you look so pensive, Doctor; speak.

Basch. We are surrounded by the enemy,
And may be beaten hopelessly to-day.

What is the object of such desp'rate fight?
What is the use to force good government
Upon a race that does not seem to care?
Unless a great majority stand firm,
And ready to defend the new regime,
You sacrifice your life and peace in vain,
We do not owe these people anything;
We came to aid them with experience
And knowledge, that on many battle fields
The older world had dearly bought with blood,
'Mid constant changes during centuries.
It seems, however, as if every state
Must gain its own experience through blood,
So let us leave them to contend and fight,
While we return to our old, peaceful home;
There, you will rule, as once, among your friends,
A blessing to them all, and blest yourself.

 Max. Yes, you are right, seen from your point of view;
For, like Diogenes, housed in his tub,
You judge the world with true philosophy,
But do not know how wounded honor galls.

 Basch. We must discern two kinds of honor, Sire:
The outward, false one, others may defile;
The inward, true one, none but our own deeds.

 Father Vischer. Then let true honor be your action's guide;
Defend your rights, whatever others think.
Great men would never have achieved success
If they had catered but to public praise;
Those who accomplish greatness, stand alone.
Think of our Lord, how faithfully he fought,

Until blind masses nailed him to the cross.
It is the mission of your Majesty
To save this country from wild anarchy,
And civilize the land through church and law.
If you fulfil this duty faithfully,
The Virgin's words will likewise be fulfilled:
"A mighty realm" will be your own at last.

Max. Yes: I must fight, and manfully hold out.
If I but had the troops and generals.

Father Vischer. Above all things, conciliate the church;
She will procure the means to raise new troops,
And, as for leaders, two of them are here:
For Marquez, just arrived, and Miramon,
They who were stricken from the army roll.

Max. What? Can it be? O, thanks to Providence.
Quick; bring them here. What unexpected luck!

Father Vischer. See, here they come.

SCENE II.

The same. MIRAMON, MARQUEZ, MEJIA and Staff.

Marquez. Your Majesty!

Miramon. My Prince!

Max. Arise. Be welcome, worthy friends in need;
You are my friends indeed; you must forget
That under pressure of some court intrigues
I was misled to lose my faith in you;

Receive again my fullest confidence,
And be once more my trusted generals.

    Marquez.   Ah, Sire, your magnanimity is great.

    Miramon.   Trust me once more, and I will prove to you
My gratitude in deeds instead of words.

    Max.   That sounds like Miramon; I know you will.
Well, you shall have the chance; on every side
We are surrounded, and the greedy foe
Expects to see anon our flag of truce;
But he shall dearly buy his victory!
You, Marquez, hurry to the Capitol;
With hundred horseman you must cut your way;
If you can hold the city till to-night,
I shall be able to relieve your force;
These charts and papers, you will find, contain
Your full instructions, and the battle's plan.
The Lord be with you!

    Marquez.   I will hurry, Sire!

    Max.   You, Miramon, shall stay about me now,
And be my trusted friend as formerly.
Forgive me, and forget my old mistake.

    Miramon.   It was forgotten long ago by me;
I am prepared to serve my Emperor,
And for his cause shed my last drop of blood.

    Max.   Thanks, Miramon; select my fleetest horse,
And take at once command upon the left,
From where I soon expect a fierce attack.
Prince Salm will give you all advice you need. [*Exit Miramon.*]

With such assistance Hapsburg cannot fail;
Instead of hoisting our white flag of truce,
Unfurl the proud imperial banner now,
As sign that we are ready for the fray.
[*To staff.*] Come, gentlemen, to yonder higher ground,
From where we can survey the battle-field.

[*Maximilian and staff go toward a height in the background.*

Scene III.

Donna Arteaga. Donna Inez. Maximilian and Staff.
Later, Messenger.

Donna Arteaga. So we must fly from home a second time,
Although my strength will hardly carry me,
Hark! there again the guns are thundering forth,
Just as they did when our brave men were slain,
And our defenceless homes were burned and wrecked.
Good luck to them if they bring that revenge
For which I pine and pray by night and day.

Inez. Do not say that; the Emp'ror was so good
And gracious to us, and he spoke to me
With kind regard, just like a citizen;
I hoped that they would hoist the flag of truce;
He, sadly smiling, promised me he would,
When I implored him for his mother's sake,
Last night when I had served his frugal meal.

Donna Arteaga.
No! Vengeance! Vengeance! Come away from here!
[*Exit both.*

Max. Mejia, look; what is that on the hill?
Can it be Juarez' flag? It is not ours.

Mejia. It is the enemy's! Our men retreat!

1st Soldier. Betrayed by Marquez! He has joined the foe!

Mejia.
What? Marquez? Man, you do not speak the truth!

1st Soldier. By all that's sacred, General, I do!
First, he rode briskly with his little band
The shortest road to reach the Capitol,
Examining his orders and his plans;
But when he found our regiments exposed,
While Juarez seemed so strong, he slowed his pace,
Spoke whisp'ring to the other officers,
Then left the road, and finally rode straight
In the direction of the hostile camp;
And I alone of all the horsemen turned,
And hurried back to bring you warning, Sire.

Max. I never shall forget your services;
The loss, however, is beyond repair;
The others in possession of our plans!
Mejia, how can such rank treason be?
To break his newly sworn allegiance thus;
And Miramon—will he betray us too?

Mejia. Not he; I know his heart; it is like gold!

2d Soldier. Send troops immediately to our left wing,
Or we will not be able to hold out.

Max. We are without a single corps to send;
The last reserves were ordered to the front.

3d Soldier. Fly! Quick, your Majesty! The center breaks!

4th Soldier. The left wing is completely beaten, Sire!
Though Miramon fought in our very midst,
Just like a lion, we were overwhelmed.
I saw him fall into the victor's hands.

Max. My horse! My sword! [*Hurries into the house.*

General. Come on! One last attempt!

SCENE IV.

The same. PORFIRIO DIAZ.

Porfirio [*from the left*]. Here! Follow me!
[*From all sides soldiers rush in fighting.*

Mejia. Now for it, man to man!

Porfirio. Hold! Do not fire! Resistance is in vain;
Save useless waste of life; give up your swords.
[*An officer takes the swords.*

Max. [*rushing in*]. Porfirio!

Porfirio. Maximilian! No! Stand back!
Place him in custody, and take his sword.

Max. [*slowly giving up his sword*].
Is this the man whom I have saved from death,
And whom I lovingly drew to my heart?
Porfirio, has the war turned you to stone?

Porfirio [*harshly*].
Away! [*Turning aside.*] O, what a painful victory!

Scene V.

Tuileries Library of 1st Scene, Act I.

Napoleon III. Druyn de Lhuys.

Druyn. I warned you, Sire, we cannot keep it up;
The papers timidly cry: "Grand success,"
But everybody knows we had to yield
To brazen threats of the United States.

Napoleon. Bah! Do not worry me; I am not well.
We were not beaten at a single point;
The troops have done their duty manfully,
And now return with fame and victory.

Druyn. Your famous uncle, when at Moscow's gate——

Napoleon. Enough! Did Satan prompt that name to you?
It seems to persecute me day and night.

Druyn. I only mean——

Napoleon.   I know it; you mean well——
Excuse my temper, and—no more to-day.
            [*Exit Druyn. Enter Jean.*]
What is it now? Am I to have no rest?

Jean. Arrived from Mexico this very day,
Empress Carlotta begs your Majesty——

Napoleon. The Empress here, in France! Impossible!
What does she want? No, no; I am not well—
I can—I will not see the woman. Go!
Has everything combined to drive me mad?

Scene VI.

Napoleon. Carlotta.

Carlotta. Stand back; I am determined to be heard!
Napoleon!

Napoleon. I am surprised, madame,
To see you here.

Carlotta. O, my imperial friend,
If you had well considered our sad fate,
And carried to the end your glorious plans,
Instead of listening to low envy's voice,
This painful task would have been spared to me.

Napoleon. I always follow out my own intents,
And I have likewise done so in your case.
However, I must ask to be excused;
I must avoid excitement; I am ill.

Carlotta. He who would rule the destinies of men,
Whose single word determines weal and woe,
He cannot be excused when on his aid
Depends an Emp'ror's and a nation's fate.

Napoleon. Well, then, I beg of you to make it short!

Carlotta. I wish I could display before your eyes
A view of Mexico in her distress; ·
It would be more impressive than all words.
While everything appears to favor us,
And we seem sure to triumph in the end,
Behold, without advice or warning word,

The troops of France are suddenly withdrawn,
And close behind them, pressing on their heels,
Come Juarez' unresisted rebel hordes.
We firmly counted on the French support,
We had a right to do so, by our pact.

   Napoleon.   It is not safe to count on unpaid troops.

   Carlotta.   The Emperor rewarded all your men,
As far as our contracted means would reach.

   Napoleon.   Who is to blame for such contracted means?
The Emperor, while he has ample time
To fill his treasury and train his troops,
Devotes himself to school laws and fine arts;
Then, blindly yielding to the Bishop's threats,
He promises to give the church-lands back,
And, in vain-glorious consciousness of power
Condemns the prisoners of war to death,—
From weakness, swaying thus to cruelty.

   Carlotta.   Where he shows energy, you call him cruel!
Where he is merciful, you call him weak;
Why, then, did you select him for your plans,
And strongly urge him to accept the crown.

   Napoleon.   I never did select nor urge him on!
The vote of Mexico elected him.

   Carlotta.   You need no longer make that false pretence;
We long have known that not the people's vote,
But that Bazaine's intrigues controlled the choice.

   Napoleon.   If he knew that—imagined that he knew—
And was so anxious for the people's weal,
Why did he not resign the worthless crown,

And leave a realm that never wanted him?
Why was my envoy, Castelnau, dismissed,
In anger, when he warned him to resign?

Carlotta. Because his honor forced him so to act.
He felt inspired, and thought he might succeed,
And lead the people on to better ways.

Napoleon. Bah! Honor, when we deal with multitudes?
No; merely his ambition blinded him;
A strong desire to deck his foolish head
A little longer with a glittering crown.

Carlotta. No further, I implore! Do not be hard!
Think how the Emperor is fighting, now,
With small support against a mighty foe;
Perhaps already captured, or—still worse—
I dare not think of it. O, send him troops!
Provide more means to carry out the work;
Fear not that proud republic's threatening voice,
Nor yet the discontent of men in France.

Napoleon [*angrily*].
I fear not foreign folks, nor those at home!

Carlotta. Then do not let me kneel here at your feet
In vain, for my poor husband,—for your friend.

Napoleon. I pray you, do not kneel, madame; arise.
I can no more deplete my treasury,
No longer sacrifice my people's blood,
To further help a crank's fantastic whims;
I must confess, I quite misjudged the man.

Carlotta. O, what a cruel, sneering, heartless tone!

And so you cannot help the faithful friend
Who fought far more for you than for himself.

Napoleon. I helped him quite enough—indeed, too much;
Now, he must help himself, or meet his fate.

Carlotta. That cannot be your final word?

Napoleon. It is!

Carlotta. O, Max! Then you are doomed without a hope!
Why did you ever trust this vicious snake,
This low deceiver, this cold-blooded wretch!

Napoleon. Control your tongue, for I will stand no more!
Your sex alone protects you from my wrath;
Do you forget, madame, to whom you speak?

Carlotta. I wish I could forget that I now stand
Before my husband's treach'rous murderer.

[*Napoleon sinks, as if paralyzed, into a chair. Carlotta tears off her diadem, and throws it at his feet.*]

Take back the crown that you have thrust on us,
And give, O give us back our happiness.
With glittering words you tempted us from home,
Incited the ambition of your friend.
In glowing tints the future was portrayed:
How certain was the French assistance then!
How cowardly were those confederates
Who wisely had withdrawn from all your plans!
What grand contempt you had for that new world
That boldly warned you not to interfere.
Alas! He yielded to your urgent wish,
And sacrificed his life and peace for you;
Then, at the moment when success seems sure,

The great republic's threats so frighten you,
That, though unbeaten, all your valiant troops
Fly from the battle-field in shameless haste.
What do you care, that countless skeletons
Lie bleaching on the bloody fields in vain?
You do not mind that now the pride of France
Will bear forever this disgraceful stain,
That by your miserable policy,
A noble friend's great heart must bleed and break.
What's that to you! Your bosom is of stone!
If there is justice still in heaven, beware!
Your time will come, when, far away from home,
Scorned and forsaken, you will die alone.
Cursed be the moment when your scheming mind
Entangled Maximilian in your plans!
Cursed be the brain that spun the vile intrigues!
Woe be to you and yours! Your name shall be
Forgotten and destroyed for evermore!
Your vicious race shall disappear from earth!
My curse on you! My curse on all your house!

Napoleon. An icy shock has paralyzed my limbs;
I cannot move; I cannot call for help!

Carlotta. You cannot call? Well, I will call for you.
[*She calls.*] Come in! Come, all of you that hear my voice!
[*Enter the Court, through various doors.*]
Come in, and see the man that I have cursed!
And now, see there—see—Maximilian—
His manly bearing and imperial brow!
But look—he bleeds—his breast is full of wounds!
No; still he fights, and leads his band of braves;

While, unconcerned, the troops of France stand by
And see him hopelessly despair! My God!
The enemy has overpowered him!—
They lead him off to execution! Help!
They fire!—my head!   [*She breaks down.*

   Napoleon [*recovering himself*]. Why do you stand and stare?
Do you not see the woman is insane?
Lead her away, and send my doctors here.
                       [*Exit Carlotta and Court.*]
O what a day! Cowed by a woman's hate!
I feel as if her curse had sealed my fate.

Scene VII.

Queretaro Cloister Vaults.

MAXIMILIAN, *at the right, sleeping in a coffin.* DR. BASCH, *at the left, his head on the table.* SCHOOLMASTER.

   Schoolmaster [*setting out bread and water*].
Yes, so it goes. Not only Art alone,
But Science, too, must stoop to work for bread;
Take me, for instance—prison warden now.
My elegance of style is sacrificed;
But times are hard, and no one cares for style.
See, there he lies, exhausted, pale as death,
A coffin all they gave him for a bed.
Who would have thought, a little while ago,
When I received him with the childrens' choir,
That I would be imperial caterer,

Doorkeeper, too, and valet, all in one.
He moves, he is awake!

Max. Where am I here?
Already in my coffin, in my vault?
Is this what we call death, and what seems life,
The soul alone, that rises, feels, and thinks?

Schoolmaster. I hope your Majesty has rested well.

Max. That is not Charon—but—who are you, man?

Schoolmaster. The prison warden of your Majesty.

Max. And these dark walls?

Schoolmaster. Are catacombs, the vaults
Of our old cloister, and your prison now;
In deep, unconscious trance they brought you here;
They could not find a better place at once.

Max. So I am further still condemned to live;
I hoped to sleep my last eternal sleep.
There is my faithful doctor—let him sleep;
He, too, is tired and worn by overwork.
Tell me, good friend, what is the news abroad?
Empress Carlotta, have they heard from her?

Schoolmaster. The prison laws, in language very strict,
Prohibit talking to the prisoners;
But that, I think, applies alone to those
Of whom repentance is expected still.

Max. Speak, my good man, what is the latest news?

Schoolmaster. It is not always safe to trust the press,
Because, you see, good reasons may prevail
For changing facts, by pressure from above.

Max. O, tell me what you know. You torture me!
For many days I have not heard from her.

Schoolmaster. The papers say no very great success
Has crowned the efforts of her Majesty;
And that, in consequence——

    Max.   Well, what?

    Schoolmaster.   That she—
Well,—bodily she has not suffered much.

Max. Poor friend, I fear you are of unsound mind.

Schoolmaster. Perhaps I am—and yet, perhaps I'm not;
And, if I were, I need no pity, Sire.
To him, bowed down and crushed by wants and cares,
Whom even Future shows no glimpse of hope,
To him it is a blessing when his mind
Is shrouded in a gentle, hazy veil,
That helps to soothe the pains of memory.

Max. How true those words, though spoken by a fool;
To hopeless misery, that cannot die,
Insanity must be a welcome friend.

    Schoolmaster. Yes; so said all who heard the Empress' fate.

    Max. "The Empress' fate?" You do not mean to say——

    Schoolmaster.
The noble mind of your good Empress is——

Max. No more! Do not pronounce that dreadful word.
My God, am I not suffering enough!

    Schoolmaster. As you divine it, I need say no more.
                                                                        [*Exit.*

    Max. O, Doctor, say it is not true!

Basch [*awakening*]. What now?

Max. It cannot be, that my beloved wife,
My poor, my gentle child, has lost her mind?

Basch. Who dared to tell your Majesty?

Max. A fool;
And fools and children speak the truth, they say.
You sigh in silence? O, my God, my God!
That breaks the thread that tied me to this life,
And reconciles me to an early death.
Will, after death, in yonder better world,
I surely meet again my darling wife?
And will her mind rise freed from darkening clouds,
As human soul throws off the mortal coil,
That I may see her as in by-gone days,
And live with her in perfect happiness?
What do you think of our eternal life?

Basch. I wish that I could give you hope and trust;
However, what we call man's life on earth
Is struggling, suffering, never-ending strife,
For that perfection which, if once attained,
Would be the end of all felicity.
On imperfection happiness depends;
To gratify our wants is greatest bliss;
Perfection has no wants to gratify.
Must not eternal life appear to us
Eternal struggle and eternal woe—
An everlasting, unrewarded strife?
It seems to me that all good souls deserve
Eternal, dreamless, and unconscious rest.

Max.   I would that I could hear the Bishop's views!

Schoolmaster.   Sire, Don Benito Juarez has arrived,
And asks to hold an interview with you.

Max.   Must I endure this, too! Well, let him come;
All cares seem trifling after my great loss.

Scene VIII.

The same. Juarez.

Juarez.   It grieves me much to find you, Hapsburg, here,
And I am sorry that you ever came,
For, when you came, your present fate was sure.

Max.   The bitter war, this iron game of dice,
Is at an end, and your's the highest throw.

Juarez.   Much better call the game an iron chess,
For all the moves were calculated well.
What good were all your castles and your knights,
While every peon stood by me alone.
You lost the Bishop early in the game,
And towards the last your noble Queen——

Max.   Enough!
Have you come here to taunt me cruelly?

Juarez.   Not that. I only wished to show how wrong,
How foolish was your venture from the start.
You surely could not entertain the hope
To build a firm, successful government
Upon foundations soaked in human blood!

Max. In peace, I would have ruled with milder hand
Than you or others ever did before.

Juarez. A people, ripe to mould their government,
Would rather yield to tyrants of their choice
Than to the mildness of a foreign prince.

Max. But just that ripeness Mexicans have not.

Juarez. You never knew, nor tried to know, these men;
You were misguided by your thirst for fame,
And you were ruled where you supposed you ruled.
If in my hands alone I held your fate,
You might go hence, return to your old home,
And live, a warning to ambitious kings;
But, as you know, court-martials are severe;
They measure you by your own measure now:
"All who are found with weapons in their hands
"Resisting law and government, shall be
"Court-martialed—executed on the spot."
Who is now "government?" Who broke that law?
 [*Takes the sentence from a soldier.*]
This is your sentence; read the words yourself:
"Mejia, Maximilian, Miramon,
"Found guilty of high treason, are condemned
"To death, and hereby sentenced to be shot."
 [*He gives the sentence to Maximilian.*

Max. Poor friends!

Juarez. You think the verdict too severe?

Max. Not for myself. I ask no better fate
Than to be judged by laws I gave myself;
But if the conquered be allowed to ask

One favor of his conqueror's good grace,
Have mercy on my faithful followers,
Who pay for their devotion with their lives;
Release Mejia, pardon Miramon,
And take my blood as ransom for us all.

   Juarez. The public is enraged beyond control;
If I should try to save your friends from death,
The people's wrath would slaughter them and me.
If I can serve you otherwise——

   Max.   No, thanks.

   Juarez. I very much regret you ever came.
The Lord be merciful to you.   Farewell!   [*Exit Juarez.*

   Max. So, then, my fate is sealed, my life is doomed.

   Basch. The friends at home will surely interfere;
And, after some resistance, they must yield.

   Max. No, nothing saves my life; my time has come.
Farewell, yon hills and valleys of my home,
My feet will tread your gentle slopes no more;
Farewell, all relatives and distant friends;
Forgive me if I ever did you wrong.
Of those who have betrayed my confidence
I will not think unkindly at my death.
O, now I comprehend the Virgin's words,
That in my vanity I misconceived:
"A mighty kingdom waits for thee," she said;
Yes, yes; the mighty kingdom of the dead!

Scene IX.

Place of execution.

Prince Iturbide. Princess Iturbide (*in distress*).

Prince Iturbide. Come, dearest aunt; come, let us go away;
Do not delay in such a fearful place.

Princess Iturbide. No; I will stay; I want to see it all.
Perhaps my overburdened heart will break,
And end the tortures of a ruined life.
Hark! Is the terrible procession near?

[*She sees Porfirio Diaz.*]

Quick! Stand aside! I fear that wicked man!

Scene X.

Procession (funeral march). Maximilian, Mejia, Miramon,
their Wives, Miramon's Children, Dr. Basch, Father
Vischer, La Bastida, Juarez, Porfirio, Soldiers,
People.

Max. O, what a lovely day, so pure and bright!
I always wished to die on such a day,
And heaven has kindly gratified my wish.
[*To Basch.*] To my old mother take this hat, these gloves,
And say they are the last that I have worn;
And she, the mother of a Hapsburg, will
Much rather see the hat without the son,
Who honorably perished at his post,

Than, with the hat, receive a son disgraced.
And my poor wife—the Lord has spared her this!

 Officer. If you desire to speak, now is the time.

 Mejia. At my ripe age, the pleasures of this life
Can have for me no more attraction now.
I have so often looked death in the face,
That all its terrors do not touch my heart.
However, I protest most solemnly,
Before the Lord and all these witnesses,
Against a court that had no right to judge,—
Not us, much less a crowned, imperial head.
You are not judges—simply murderers:
This consciousness shall follow you till death;
Confound your thoughts with guilty shame by day,
And rouse your fears with ghastly dreams by night,
When by your beds we rise in bloody shrouds
And shake our warning hands in mournful threat;
Thus you will be far more condemned than we,
Who peacefully repose from work and strife.
I feel my conscience free! On you my blood!

 Miramon. The old may have a just contempt for life;
But I am young! I have my wife and child:
Be merciful, and pardon my misdeeds,
That I may further care for those I love,
For they must starve, unless I can provide.
I promise, and I swear upon my oath,
To never raise my hand against this State.
We all will wander far away from here,
And seek a home in distant foreign lands.

      [*He takes the child's hand.*]

What are all realms to me, compared to this
One tiny finger of this little hand!
Oh! Do not let me die! Pray let me live!
Spare me! O, spare me! for the sake of these!

    Max. We all must die, poor friend; there is no hope.

    Officer. Your pardon, Majesty: forgive me, all,
That I must be your executioner.

    Max. You are a soldier, and you must obey;
Give me your hand, and do your duty then.
And you [*to Soldiers*], accept my last, though trifling gift,
[*gives money*] And aim, I beg of you, right at the heart.
To all of you, who have come out to-day
To be the witnesses of our near death,
I swear to you, and call the Lord above
To witness that I tried to serve you well;
And, whether cruel I appeared, or weak,
I had at heart the welfare of the State.
I much regret that I had not the chance
To prove to you by deeds these sentiments;
Believe my word, then, in this solemn hour,
That my intentions have been pure and just;
And if great Providence, that guides us all,—
If history, or the development
Of Mexico, demanded this ordeal,
I am prepared to sacrifice my life.
O, how I wish this blood might be the last
That must be shed for this afflicted land!
And may these acres, fertilized with blood,
Produce, some day, three flowers rich and rare—

The flowers' names are: "Justice, Freedom, Peace!"
Could I take that conviction to my grave,
I would give up my life most readily
For my beloved second fatherland,
Which I have learned to love in short success
And long distress. Farewell to all of you.
Hurrah for freedom! Long live Mexico!

> [*Maximilian, Mejia and Miramon are led off into the wings to be executed. Peal of bells.*

Basch. Have mercy! Pardon them! Still there is time!

Father Vischer.
O, do not judge, that you may not be judged.

Juarez. I do not judge, and he is not condemned;
The spirit of the times dooms tyranny.
Let tyrants rule old worlds beyond the sea,
The new world glories in her liberty.

> [*La Bastida raises the crucifix. The officer raises and drops his sword, instead of verbal command. Three volleys are fired, while the curtain drops.*

THE END.

www.ingramcontent.com/pod-product-compliance
Lightning Source LLC
Chambersburg PA
CBHW031408160426
43196CB00007B/945